Talk to Her

Pedro Almodóvar is one of the most renowned film directors of recent years. *Talk to Her* (*Hable con ella*) is one of the most discussed and controversial of all his films. Dealing principally with the issue of rape, it also offers profound insights into the nature of love and friendship while raising important philosophical and moral questions in unsettling and often paradoxical ways.

This is the first book to explore and address the philosophical aspects of Almodóvar's film. Opening with a helpful introduction by Noël Carroll that places the film in context, specially commissioned chapters examine the following topics:

- The relationship between art and morality and the problem of "immoralism"
- Moral injury and its role in the way we form moral judgments, including the ethics of love and friendship
- The nature of dialogue, sexual objectification and what "listening to" means in the context of gender
- Almodóvar's use of allusion and the unmasking of appearances to explore hidden themes in human nature.

Including a biography of Almodóvar, *Talk to Her* is essential reading for students interested in philosophy and film as well as ethics and gender. It also provides an accessible and informative insight into philosophy for those in related disciplines such as film studies, literature, and religion.

Contributors: Noël Carroll, A.W. Eaton, Cynthia Freeland, Robert B. Pippin, C.D.C. Reeve, and George M. Wilson.

A.W. Eaton is Assistant Professor of Philosophy at the University of Illinois at Chicago. She has published articles on the relationship between ethics and aesthetics, pornography, and feminist aesthetics.

Philosophers on Film

The true significance of film for philosophy, and of philosophy for film, cannot be established in abstract or general terms. It can only be measured in and through individual philosophers' attempts to account for their experience of specific films. This series promises to provide a productive context for that indispensable enterprise.

Stephen Mulhall, Fellow and Reader in
Philosophy, New College, Oxford

Film is increasingly used to introduce and discuss key topics and problems in philosophy, whilst some films raise important philosophical questions of their own. Yet until now, dependable resources for those studying and teaching philosophy and film have been limited. Philosophers on Film answers this growing need and is the first series of its kind.

Each volume assembles a team of international contributors who explore a single film in depth. Beginning with an introduction by the editor, each specially-commissioned chapter discusses a key aspect of the film in question. Additional features include a biography of the director and suggestions for further reading, making the series ideal for anyone studying philosophy, film and anyone with a general interest in the philosophical dimensions of cinema.

Forthcoming:

- *The Thin Red Line*, edited by David Davies
- *Eternal Sunshine of the Spotless Mind*, edited by Christopher Grau
- *Memento*, edited by Andrew Kania
- *Blade Runner*, edited by Amy Coplan

Talk to Her

Edited by

A.W. Eaton

Routledge
Taylor & Francis Group

LONDON AND NEW YORK

This edition published 2009
by Routledge
2 Park Square, Milton Park, Abingdon, Oxon, OX14 4RN

Simultaneously published in the USA and Canada
by Routledge
711 Third Ave, New York, NY 10017

Routledge is an imprint of the Taylor & Francis Group, an informa business

Typeset in Joanna by
Florence Production Ltd, Stoodleigh, Devon

British Library Cataloguing in Publication Data
A catalogue record for this book is available from the British Library

Library of Congress Cataloging in Publication Data
Talk to Her / edited by Anne Eaton.
    p. cm.—(Philosophers on film)
    Includes bibliographical references and index.
    1. Hable con ella (Motion picture).   2. Almodóvar, Pedro.
    3. Motion pictures—Moral and ethical aspects.   I. Eaton, Anne
    (Anne Wescott).
    PN1997.2.H33T35 2008
    791.43′72—dc22   2008010507

ISBN 10: 0–415–77366–0 (hbk)
ISBN 10: 0–415–77367–9 (pbk)

ISBN 13: 978–0–415–77366–9 (hbk)
ISBN 13: 978–0–415–77367–6 (pbk)

Contents

Illustrations

All illustrations in this volume are reproduced from *Talk to Her*, Dir. Pedro Almodóvar (2002).

Acknowledgments

This volume grew out of a session on Almodóvar at the Central Division meeting of the American Philosophical Association, April 2005. Heartfelt thanks to Louise Antony for making this session possible. Without her encouragement this volume would not exist. The editor would also like to thank Tony Bruce for his vision in organizing this valuable series and the others at Routledge for their help in producing this volume. Finally the editor would like to thank the contributors for their patience and, more important, for their excellent essays.

Contributor biographies

Noël Carroll is a distinguished professor at the Graduate Center of the City University of New York. His most recent publication is *The Philosophy of Motion Pictures* (2008). His forthcoming publications include *On Criticism* (Routledge, 2009) and *The Philosophy of Art of Arthur Danto*.

A.W. Eaton is an Assistant Professor in Philosophy at the University of Illinois at Chicago. She has published articles on the relationship between ethics and aesthetics, pornography, and feminist aesthetics. In addition to these topics, she is currently working on issues in value theory and artifact function, and is writing a book on ethics and the pictorial arts. She was a Laurance Rockefeller Fellow at Princeton's Center for Human Values in 2005–6 and previously taught at Bucknell University.

Cynthia Freeland is Professor and Chair of Philosophy at the University of Houston. Her previous work on aesthetics includes *Philosophy and Film* (co-edited with Tom Wartenberg), *The Naked and the Undead: Evil and the Appeal of Horror*, and *But Is It Art?* She also writes on topics in feminist theory and ancient philosophy.

Robert B. Pippin is the Evelyn Stefansson Nef Distinguished Service Professor in the Committee on Social Thought, the Department of Philosophy, and the College at the University of Chicago. He is the author of several books on German idealism, including *Kant's Theory of Form*; *Hegel's Idealism: The Satisfactions of Self-Consciousness*, and *Modernism as a Philosophical Problem*. His latest books are *Henry James and Modern Moral Life*; a collection of his recent essays in German, *Die Verwirklichung der Freiheit*; a collection of recent essays, *The Persistence of Subjectivity*; and *Nietzsche, moraliste français*. His research interests include Kant, German Idealism, moral and political theory, contemporary European philosophy, modernity theory, philosophy and literature, and theories of freedom. He is a winner of the Mellon Distinguished Achievement Award in the Humanities, a member of the American Academy of Arts and Sciences, and was recently a fellow at the Wissenschaftskolleg zu Berlin.

C.D.C. Reeve is Delta Kappa Epsilon Distinguished Professor of Philosophy at the University of North Carolina at Chapel Hill. His books include *Philosopher-Kings* (1988, reissued 2006), *Socrates in the Apology* (1989), *Practices of Reason* (1995), *Aristotle: Politics* (1998), *Plato: Cratylus* (1998), *The Trials of Socrates* (2002), *Substantial Knowledge* (2003), *Plato: Republic* (2005), *Love's Confusions* (2005), and *Plato on Love* (2006). He is also contributing to the volumes on *Blade Runner* and *Eternal Sunshine of the Spotless Mind* in the present series.

George Wilson is Professor of Philosophy and Cinematic Arts at the University of Southern California. He has also taught at Johns Hopkins and the University of California at Davis. He has written a book on film, *Narration in Light* (Johns Hopkins Press, 1986), and a book on theory of action, *The Intentionality of Human Action* (Stanford University Press, 1989). He has published articles in the philosophy of language, theory of action, philosophy of mind, Wittgenstein, and the aesthetics of film and literature.

Note on the director

Pedro Almodóvar was born in 1949 in the small Spanish town of Calzada de Calatrava. Acknowledging the early influence of directors such as Alfred Hitchcock, Luis Buñuel, and Federico Fellini he has said that "cinema became my real education, much more than the one I received from the priest."

In 1967 he moved to Madrid in the hope of becoming a film director to discover that Franco had closed the National School of Cinema. Almodóvar instead worked for Telefonica, Spain's national phone company, for twelve years as an administrative assistant. He became a central figure in Madrid's *La Movida Madrilena Movement*, a cultural renaissance that followed the fall of Franco, and began to write articles for major Spanish newspapers and magazines such as *El País*, *Diario 16* and *La Luna*.

His first major film, *What Have I Done to Deserve This?* (1984), introduced themes that were to characterize much of his later work, in particular those of the downtrodden yet resourceful housewife, sexual identity, and the dynamics of comically dysfunctional families. This was followed by *Women on the Verge of a Nervous Breakdown* (1988), *Tie Me Up! Tie Me Down!* (1990), *Talk to Her* (2002), *Bad Education* (2004), and *Volver* (2006). A hallmark of Almodóvar's richly creative work is his depiction of controversial themes in occasionally graphic and violent style, a method that has attracted considerable criticism in his homeland. Almodóvar has passionately defended artistic freedom, stating that "the moral of my films is to get to a greater stage of freedom."

He is the most successful and internationally known Spanish filmmaker of his generation. *All About My Mother* (1999) has received more awards and honors than any other film in the Spanish motion picture industry, including an Oscar for Best Foreign Language Film, a Golden Globe in the same category, and a Best Director and Ecumenical Award at Cannes.

Chapter 1

Noël Carroll

TALK TO THEM:
AN INTRODUCTION

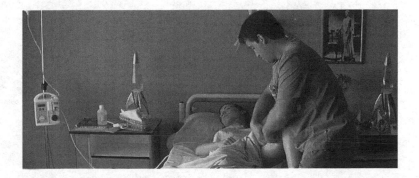

E VER SINCE THE PUBLICATION OF Stanley Cavell's *The World Viewed* in 1972, the volume of dialogue about motion pictures in the world of English-speaking philosophy has been increasing at a geometrical rate. There are now quite a number of undergraduate textbooks that use movies to introduce students to the classical problems of philosophy. Anthologies abound entitled *Philosophy and* ———, where the blank is filled in with the name of some popular culture franchise, and often that of a motion picture or a motion picture maker. Indeed, at last count, three publishers were trolling in this market.

There is an academic journal devoted to the subject, called Film and Philosophy, which is connected to a society—the Society for the Philosophical Study of Contemporary Visual Art—whose sessions are predominantly concerned with film. Books and articles on cinema by philosophers are appearing at a steady pace and courses in philosophy and film are spreading like wildfire. And now Routledge has launched this splendid new series devoted to the philosophical examination of individual films of note.

One reason for the explosion of interest in cinema on the part of philosophers has to do with the fact that baby-boomers and subsequent generations have grown up in a culture saturated with moving pictures, not only in theaters, but, perhaps even more importantly, on television. Motion pictures are everywhere, from hospital waiting rooms and airport lounges to your computer and your cell phone. It would be astounding if such an enormous part of culture escaped the notice of philosophy. Moreover, motion pictures form such a "natural" or, at least, presumed part of the lives of the students in philosophy classes that it is predictable that their teachers would attempt to take advantage of this fact.

The interest that philosophers are taking in motion pictures is various. There is what we may call the philosophy of motion pictures. This involves the philosophical examination of the concepts that organize the practices of motion picture-making and movie-going. Many of the questions that it addresses were once in the domain of what was called "film theory." They include: "What is cinema?," "What is the relation of film to reality?," "What is the relation of movies to the other arts?," "Is cinematic representation distinctive?," and so forth. The philosophy of the motion picture also examines the special problems of the various movie genres, such as suspense, horror, melodrama, and comedy. And, as well, the philosophy of motion pictures grapples with the moral philosophy of cinema.

However, another aspect of philosophy's interest in the movies is what I shall refer to as a concern with philosophy "in" film. As the preposition in suggests, this involves the interpretation of various motion pictures in terms of the standing philosophical themes that they can be shown to illustrate, adumbrate, or articulate, as one might find egoism exemplified by the television series The Sopranos.

Closely related to the enterprise of excavating philosophical themes from motion pictures is what we might label philosophy through motion pictures. Proponents of this view, which many find highly controversial, believe that some motion pictures do philosophy—that is, some motion pictures may offer significant contributions or insights to the conversation of philosophy. In this volume on Pedro Almodóvar's *Talk to Her*, the essayists provide examples of all three of the preceding types of philosophical engagement with cinema, often in the same article, along with extremely nuanced readings of the narrative and profoundly probing examinations of the characters.

In her piece "Almodóvar's Immoralism," A.W. Eaton addresses a current issue in the moral philosophy of the arts: the question of whether an artwork, in this case a motion picture, can advance a morally compromised viewpoint in such a way that it enhances the overall artistic value of the work. This question has emerged in the wake of recent discussions on the inadequacy of autonomism—the view that ethics and aesthetics are separate and non-intersecting realms of value such that an ethical defect in a work never lowers the aesthetic value of the work nor does the ethical merit of a work increase its aesthetic worth. Recently this view has been challenged, and several arguments have been advanced to the effect that *sometimes* an ethical flaw can contribute to the aesthetic demerit of a work. But these arguments, in turn, have led to speculation about whether or not an ethical flaw could in some other cases augment the aesthetic excellence of the work. This view has come to be called "immoralism" and Eaton maintains that *Talk to Her* confirms the possibility of immoralism.

The film tells the story of Benigno, a male nurse who attends a comatose patient named Alicia, a ballet dancer to whom Benigno was obsessively attracted even before she was involved in the automobile accident that reduced her to an almost vegetative state. Benigno, whose name means "benign" in Spanish, appears to be an immensely gentle and dedicated caregiver. He doesn't—as others might be prone to do—forget Alicia's personhood. He talks to her as if she could respond and acts as if she does. He also urges his friend Marco to treat likewise his ex-lover Lydia (who is also in a coma in the same hospital as Alicia as a result of a bullfighting mishap).

Although Benigno strikes us as not exactly mentally sound, he is otherwise presented as an extremely humane person, even perhaps somewhat saintly—a holy fool of sorts—at times. But, in the course of the story, we learn that Benigno rapes Alicia off-screen and impregnates her. Nevertheless, Eaton notes that the moral heinousness of Benigno's deed never strikes the viewer with the force that it deserves. Its impact has been aesthetically muted by Almodóvar. Reviewers, for example, treat the film as if the relation between Benigno and Alicia was a romance, albeit of the l'amour fou variety.

However, this is nothing short of ethical obfuscation, indeed, an instance of the enduring moral category error that assimilates rape as a form of love. In short, we are being led by the film to be more sympathetic and forgiving of Benigno than we should be. Our attitude towards him is morally defective, since it depends, as Eaton remarks, "upon our interpreting the rape as something other than a rape."

Furthermore, it is no accident that we have this attitude toward Benigno. It has been engineered by the filmmaker Pedro Almodóvar who, among other things, has kept the rape scene offscreen and displaced its violence and brutality onto an ostensibly unintentionally comic silent film, called The Shrinking Lover, and a bubbling lava lamp. Out of sight, out of mind. What we are left with is the appearance of Benigno's consistently kindly demeanor, which inclines us, like the movie critics, to overlook the gravity of his transgression. Thus, the film is morally defective because it both mandates that we adopt an ethically wrong attitude toward Benigno and seduces us, in large measure, into doing so.

But, Eaton adds, this moral defect redounds to the artistic merit of Talk to Her, thereby supporting the contention that immoralism is possible. According to Eaton, although the film encourages a morally pernicious viewpoint, it does not let us forget entirely that Benigno has done something terrible. Thus, on her account, the sensitive viewer is "torn between feelings of sympathy and antipathy, attraction and disgust, praise and blame," and the experience of this dilemma is salutary. Consequently, it is precisely by making us feel what we ought not to feel that the film succeeds artistically in provoking our acknowledgment of this human possibility through our own experience.

Of course, whether or not this counts in favor of immoralism hinges to a great extent upon whether or not you feel that the discovery that Almodóvar's film affords is an ethical one; an enlargement, say, of our comprehension of human possibilities that are relevant to the moral life. That is, what if it is convincing to hypothesize that Almodóvar's purpose is to thrust us into an ethically uncomfortable position for the moral purpose of revealing to us something about the natural dispositions of the human heart?

Like Eaton, Robert B. Pippin, in his paper "Devils and angels in Almodóvar's *Talk to Her*," is struck by the viewer's response to Benigno—specifically by our hesitation over simply condemning him and leaving it at that. Although the audience does not lose sight of the fact in the fiction that Benigno has done something grievously wrong, our judgment of Benigno does not end there. That Benigno is a rapist (period, full stop) is not our ultimate view of him. For, in addition, on Pippin's accounting, we also admire something about Benigno—namely his single-minded authenticity; his integrity; his wholehearted, uncompromising embrace of his existential commitments. As Pippin observes, "Benigno, for all of his delusions, retains some sort of aesthetically admirable genuineness [an integratedness?] throughout the film, an aesthetic genuineness, I would say, that we want to count as morally relevant."

Thus, in Pippin's view, *Talk to Her* affords an opportunity for philosophical insight. It leads the viewer to the recognition that questions of moral injury are not the only considerations that may come into play when engaging in moral judgment, nor should they be taken as automatically trumping all other sorts of evaluations of acts or persons. So whereas Eaton maintains that *Talk to Her* inveigles the audience to embrace an improper moral attitude, Pippin implicitly rejoins that the attitude is rather, from the moral point of view, justifiably a more commodious one—one that takes into account the admirable ways in which Benigno is true to himself.

In George M. Wilson's "Rapport, rupture, and rape: reflections on *Talk to Her*," further details are added to the portrait of what is admirable about Benigno. For Wilson, Benigno is an exemplar of a kind of fundamental human virtue. That virtue can be marked by the slogan "talk to her;" "understood in the appropriate expanded sense, [it] is a prime instance of and a metonymy for the activity of taking care of another person with unquestioning love, without any conditions and without expectations of reward or immediate response." Indeed, it is when Marco is able to talk to the dead Benigno, standing at the foot of his grave, that we come to suppose that Marco may finally be capable of love.

Of course, Wilson, like Pippin, does not think that Benigno's virtues in this regard exculpate the terrible wrong that he has committed.

Rather, Wilson argues that the philosophical lesson the film advances is that our judgment of the moral injury he has inflicted upon Alicia should not obliterate other aspects of our sympathetic response to Benigno.

Our responses to Benigno, as with many of our moral experiences outside of the cinema, are conflicted. However, we should not repress that conflict, but struggle to keep straight in our minds the considerations in which those conflicts are rooted. That too is an integral part of leading a moral life and, insofar as Talk to Her, invites—indeed encourages—viewers to cultivate this moral insight, it may not present a clear-cut victory for the immoralists.

If Wilson finds that Benigno exemplifies the virtue of "talking to her," Cynthia Freeland, in her article "Nothing is simple," reminds us that talking to her is not enough. From the perspective of feminist philosophy, Freeland notes that men must also listen to women and, if that is impossible, they must at least strive to interpret them. For, had Benigno interpreted Alicia's wishes—had he taken them seriously—he would never have violated her.

For Freeland, Talk to Her points the way toward an advance in philosophical understanding. Feminist philosophy has emphasized objectification—viewing another human being as an object rather than as a subject—as a primary lever of sexism. And, by talking to her, Benigno signals that he regards Alicia as a person rather than as a mere body, a mere thing. Yet the film "suggests that there is more to our duties than just this, since Benigno clearly does see his patient as a person." That "more," Freeland hypothesizes, using the film as a philosophical springboard, is that we must also listen to the other, interpret the other—that is, take their needs and desires to heart. Inasmuch as Benigno has no conception of Alicia's wants, he fails to live up to his moral responsibilities to her, and, by extension, so too do those of us who only talk at the other with no effort to hear and to interpret them—just as Marco fails to listen to Lydia in the car after Angela's wedding.

Freeland uses Talk to Her as a means for advancing a feminist, philosophical insight. Her interpretation of the film is what Gadamer called an "application." She derives the significance of the film from her own present dialogical context, which is feminist philosophy. She engages the film as a philosophical companion, as an opportunity to stimulate a philosophical discovery. The film presents us with a problem: insofar as Benigno appears to acknowledge Alicia's personhood, what has gone wrong here? This prompts Freeland, in turn, to conjecture that there is a need to listen and to interpret the other; talking to or at another is not sufficient.

Although Benigno gives every appearance of acknowledging Alicia as a person, Freeland goes beneath the surface to find something amiss and to specify it. In his "A celemín of shit: comedy and deception in Almodóvar's Talk to Her," C.D.C. Reeve, similarly, makes the unmasking of appearances, perhaps the most ancient subject of philosophy (dear to Plato and Hindu philosophy alike), the central theme of his explication of the film. Through various devices and on many levels, Reeve sensitively points out Almodóvar's recurring allusions—visual, verbal, narratological, and symbolic—to comely outsides that cover up black, smelly things inside, things whose emblem Reeve associates with feces. Benigno's outward appearance of innocence and naiveté, for instance, is a façade, disguising ultimately sordid desires.

For Reeve, whose approach to the film evinces the influence of psychoanalysis, the philosophy of Talk to Her is, among other things, Freudian in its affirmation of the dark underside of human nature. Reeve carefully examines the characters, revealing the psychological damage that festers within them. Reeve shows, for example, that Benigno's upbringing, dominated by his mother's nearly unprecedented dependency upon his caretaking—she's merely lazy (and depressed), rather than ill—inexorably undercuts the possibility of anything like a normal relation between Benigno and a woman. Interestingly, moreover, Reeve's views of the characters in Talk to Her echo Eaton's view of the film itself as something artistically shining on the outside that succeeds precisely by camouflaging the evil within.

My own opinion is that Talk to Her is an example of the category of philosophy through the motion picture. It is a challenge to our almost automatic tendencies when it comes to issuing ethical judgments and it functions as an occasion for deepening our appreciation of the complexity of moral judgment.

There are a number of variables that may come into play when judging an action from a moral point of view. Typically, we think that first, the action is wrong; second, the agent is blameworthy; and third, it would be better had the action not occurred. These three judgments usually cohere as a neat package, or, at least, it is our default assumption that they are of a piece. When we hear that a child has been molested our natural disposition is to presume that the action was evil, that the perpetrator is at fault, and that it would be better had the event never happened.

Talk to Her, on the other hand, complicates this line of response. The action is presented as unequivocally wrong. Yet I think we are very uncertain about whether or not Benigno is fully blameworthy, since he appears to be so mentally confused. As C.D.C. Reeve demonstrates so adeptly, Benigno's sequestered youth with his demanding and depressive mother hardly prepared him for adult relationships with the opposite sex.

Furthermore, Benigno seems, quite frankly, out of touch with reality. His belief that he has a better relationship with Alicia than most married couples have with each other is an utter fantasy, since in fact he has no interpersonal relationship with Alicia whatsoever. So although the act is evil, the degree to which we are prone to attribute blame to Benigno is tempered. Indeed, some viewers may even feel that Benigno is not guilty by virtue of insanity, and think that rather than being imprisoned he should be institutionalized. But in any event, most, I hazard, feel sadness toward Benigno rather than moral indignation.

As a result of his rape of Alicia, Alicia gives birth to a child. The child dies in the process, but the shock of the event seems to draw Alicia out of her coma. It revives her, and she is able to take up her life again. Thus, although the rape is evil, good almost miraculously results from it. We usually think of an evil event that no good can come of it—that it would be better had it never occurred. However, in *Talk to Her*, the rape—though clearly marked as immoral—is given in the fiction as the cause of Alicia's "rebirth." Consequently, I think that we hesitate in declaring that it would be better had it never happened at all. Would even Alicia want things to be otherwise if she could have been informed of the eventual outcome of the rape ahead of time?

Talk to Her is an unsettling film because of the way in which it splits apart the tidy, coordinated, negative set of verdicts that we typically issue when morally condemning an act, its agent, and its consequences. *Talk to Her* puts us in the unfamiliar position of feeling the pressure to vote for a mixed decision. Moreover, in so doing, the film invites the viewer to scrutinize the habits of thought and feeling that govern her moral judgments, thereby enabling her to understand them more precisely.

The film has the capacity, in a manner of speaking, to lead the audience from reflex to reflection, which, from my perspective, indicates that it stands with the angels rather than the devils. That it encourages philosophical self-reflection upon the workings of our moral machinery in a way that is apt to refine and improve our powers of ethical judgment, furthermore, is part of what makes the film the excellent work of art that it is.

Talk to Her philosophizes through cinema in the sense that it prompts the viewer who is ready to engage with the film to a recognition about the internal structure of moral judgment about which, if he was aware of it at all, he was only dimly aware. The film becomes a passage to moral clarity. As many authors in this volume point out, the last words of the film, uttered by Katerina, the ballet instructress, are "nothing is simple." Nothing could serve as a better observation concerning the film's point of view with respect to moral judgment.

Undoubtedly, it may sound strange to many to suggest that philosophy can be engendered through film. On the one hand, some will argue that a motion picture can't prove its case, and, without proof, there is no philosophy. On the other hand, it may be maintained that the philosophical insight that I claim for *Talk to Her* is too obvious to count as a contribution to philosophy. Hasn't everyone always realized that we may be driven toward mixed verdicts when morally assessing an act, its agent, and its consequences?

The short answer to the last question is "no"—not everyone is aware of this, or, at least, it is easy for us to forget it when caught up, especially, in the heat of moral judgment. Moreover, the kinds of philosophy in which artworks traffic are not the specialized topics of the graduate seminar (as appropriate as those are in their place). Art, especially the arts of the moving image, are aimed at a much broader audience, and the philosophy dispensed there is popular philosophy. What appears unsophisticated in an advanced class in the phenomenology of moral experience may be a revelation to the plain viewer in the local cinema.

Furthermore, it is not obvious that the title of genuine philosophy should be restricted to only insights that are new under the sun. For one function of philosophy, it seems fair to say, is to remind us of things we may know in some sense but which we have conveniently forgotten or even repressed. Isn't this, for example, what Heidegger does when he discloses the inveterate human tendency to ignore the inevitability of death? We all know that we will die, and yet most of us live our lives as if there will always be another day. Heidegger tells us what we already know, but his insights are still philosophical because we so easily fall into denial about the fact of death.

Likewise, the concluding incantation of Oedipus Rex—"Call no man happy until he is dead"—told the ancient Greeks something that they already knew about the fragility of goodness: that catastrophe can cut down a good person at any moment and that the possibilities for a reversal of fortune surround us on all sides. And yet how many live their lives as if they were cognizant of this? Instead, most plunge ahead heedlessly. In this context, Oedipus Rex is a sobering exercise in popular philosophy, a profound reminder of a truth of which the majority lose sight as they pursue their lives almost recklessly.

Similarly, the philosophizing in Talk to Her is of the popular variety. The motion picture induces insight into the nature of moral judgment for, shall we say, the lay audience. And it does so by reminding them of something that, even if they know it vaguely, they can come to know and to grasp more clearly by thinking their way through what is morally uncomfortable about their reaction to Talk to Her.

But, the skeptic may retort, even popular philosophy must involve proof if it is to count as philosophy, and there is no proof in Talk to Her. And that is literally true; we hear no demonstration propounded in the film. However, the skeptic may be looking in the wrong place for the proof that he requires. For although the motion picture, strictly speaking, does not supply the proof, it provokes and guides the audience in such a way that the thoughtful viewer herself supplies the missing proof.

Just as Socrates maeiutically educes geometry from the slave boy, Almodóvar coaxes his thesis from the spectator by setting in motion a series of events that evoke a troubled response which, when examined under the tutelage of the film, yields a more exact understanding of the vagaries of moral judgment. The proof, in other words, is to be found in us, in our experience of the film, and in our coming to terms with that experience.

Needless to say, this is hardly the final word on the matter. The skeptic will have something else to say. Nor is it the final word on the philosophical significance of Talk to Her. For philosophy is a dialogue, as the differing viewpoints about Talk to Her in this volume show so wonderfully. So enter the conversation. Read them. Engage them. Talk to them.

Chapter 2

A.W. Eaton

ALMODÓVAR'S IMMORALISM

IT MAY SURPRISE YOU THAT RAPE is almost never mentioned in the many reviews of Almodóvar's *Talk to Her*. Instead, reviewers continually refer to Benigno and Alicia as a "couple" and to their relationship as a "love affair."[1] These two things go hand in hand, of course, for it would be grossly inappropriate to refer to a rapist and his victim as a "couple" and to their interaction as a "love affair," even if, as in this case, the rapist loved his victim very much. It is surprising that reviewers fail to mention rape because it stands at the pivotal center of the film's drama; as significant as it is that Benigno talks to Alicia, it is equally significant that he *rapes* her, two acts that are importantly dissimilar in ways that I shall explain.

How are we to account for this remarkable oversight? When one stands back from the film's viewpoint and surveys the facts of the matter, there is no question that Benigno rapes Alicia. She is, after all, in a state of profound and purportedly irrecoverable unconsciousness; she is unable to give consent to anything, including sex. When a woman passes out from drinking too much and a man takes advantage of her unconscious state to have intercourse with her, that counts as rape, not because he used force but because she did not consent. It does not matter whether she is his girlfriend or a stranger, whether he loves her or takes care of her; to have intercourse with someone without her consent is to rape her.

Not only is Alicia unable to consent to sexual intercourse with Benigno, but we have good reason to believe that she would not so consent were she conscious. Even before Alicia's near-fatal accident, her waking interaction with Benigno could hardly be described as affectionate, much less loving. In a scene that foreshadows his non-consensual entry into her body later in the film, Benigno intrudes uninvited into Alicia's bedroom, fondling and stealing one of her belongings—a hairclip. Her fright upon discovering him as she emerges undressed from the shower is a clear indication, both to us and to Benigno, that he is utterly unwelcome in her intimate space.

When we consider the facts of the narrative, it seems obvious that Benigno is first a stalker, then a rapist, and that Alicia is his innocent victim. But if this is obvious, what explains the repeated failure to so much as mention rape? Why do so many critics refer to this as a "love story?" In what sense do this rapist and his victim make a couple?

I do not believe that this oversight is chiefly due to negligence on the part of reviewers. Rather, I suggest that the temptation to use the language of consensual love to describe the principal drama emanates from the film itself. In a variety of ways that I describe below, the film works to shape both our perception of and our emotional responses to Benigno, his relationship to Alicia, and his sexual act. Here are the sorts of things I have in mind.

First, Benigno's loving devotion to Alicia is the focus of the film's attention. We see him repeatedly go far beyond the call of his nursely duties to pamper her: he tones and oils her body, dresses her in crisp white linens, does her make-up and hair, impeccably manicures her hands and feet, decorates her room, and brings her thoughtful presents. His attentive care is so much the focus of the movie that it becomes difficult to conceive of him harming her. We might not have believed him when he proclaimed "I'm harmless" to a half-naked and frightened Alicia emerging from the shower, but after observing his tireless and devoted ministering to her for four years, he appears as gentle and harmless as his name suggests. "Benigno," after all, is Spanish for "benign."

Second, Benigno considers Alicia and himself to be a couple and the film explicitly adopts his point of view. "We get along better than most married couples," he tells Marco. This is, of course, a case of gross misperception on his part, for Benigno just doesn't know what a couple is (and by the way, Marco tells him so). Alicia is nothing more than a blank screen for the projection of Benigno's fantasies and he appears to neither desire nor expect that the relationship should be in the least reciprocal, a feature that becomes disastrous when he takes things to a sexual level. The difficulty for the viewers is that at many points the film aligns itself with Benigno's woefully distorted point of view. This is made explicit when, just after the ballet mistress leaves the two on the balcony, the words "Benigno y Alicia" appear on the screen. It is the same formulation in the same purple font that informed us earlier of Marco and Lydia's romantic involvement. This extra-diegetic element explicitly instructs the viewer to consider Benigno and Alicia as a couple, as a "pareja" to use the term that Almodóvar constantly employs in his commentary on the film.

Third, it is especially significant, as the film's title tells us, that Benigno *talks to* Alicia. This aligns him with the only other person who talks to her, namely the adoring ballet mistress. Talking is a sign of their love and care. But it's not just that. When everyone else appears to have given up on Alicia, Benigno and the ballet mistress continue to treat her as a person. They do not leave her to rot like a dying sack of flesh but instead acknowledge her personhood and treat her as a subject. In this way, talking to Alicia is a sign not only of care and love, but also of recognition and respect.

But if talking to Alicia dignifies her by recognizing her subjectivity, rape accomplishes precisely the opposite. Rape is an act of subordination that objectifies, degrades, and humiliates its victims. How, in anyone's eyes, could Benigno's talking to Alicia overshadow the fact that he takes complete advantage of his position and her helplessness to use her as a means to his sexual ends? The answer has everything to do with the way that the sexual intercourse is represented. Or, rather, *not* represented.

As one reviewer puts it, the act itself is "blessedly . . . not shown."[2] Instead, we see Benigno preparing to give Alicia a massage (purportedly because he worries that she might get the flu). It is night time and Alicia is fully made up in lipstick, eye shadow and pigtails, as if ready for a date. Benigno is in a noticeably disturbed state as he begins to undress her. He uncovers her breasts, affording the viewer an erotic glimpse, but then recovers them and sits down to gather himself. "No, I'm all right," he tells her, as if she'd inquired about his well-being, but this reciprocation is, as always, imagined—she never stirs from her motionless, vegetative state. He then begins to massage her hands and to tell her about a silent movie he saw the night before entitled "Shrinking Lover."

We then cut to the movie itself which is in the style of a 1920s' black and white art film. It tells the story of Amparo, a scientist, and her boyfriend, Alfredo, who drinks her experimental diet formula, which causes him to shrink to the height of a few centimeters.

After recounting some of the trials and tribulations attending Alfredo's severely diminished size, the camera cuts back to Benigno and Alicia. We see Alicia, her breasts again uncovered, almost exactly from Benigno's optical standpoint as he begins to massage her torso and hips with both hands. His breathing becomes more labored and the massage takes on an increasingly sexual tone.

The camera then cuts back to the silent movie. Amparo and the miniature Alfredo arrive at a hotel and are in bed together talking. She then falls asleep and he, in a gesture similar to Benigno's in the previous scene, pulls back the sheet to slowly and tantalizingly reveal her breasts. Alfredo then climbs onto her breast and makes his way down her body to her seemingly enormous vagina into which he eventually crawls. The last shot of the silent movie is a close-up of Amparo's face in an expression of sexual ecstasy.

Drawing an explicit parallel, the camera then cuts to Alicia's face from the same distance. Next we see Benigno in a noticeably aroused state massaging her thighs. He tells Alicia, with an excited and labored breath, that Alfredo remains inside Amparo forever. The camera then cuts to a close-up shot of the lava lamp that sits beside Alicia's bed. We see soft, rounded forms the color of blood gently separate and recombine in a lovely viscous flow.

This sequence—from the moment Alfredo begins to uncover Amparo's naked sleeping body to the shot of the lava lamp—is unified by music. It is a romantic piece in a minor key whose main theme winds gently through the registers of the strings. After its climax at the moment of Amparo's expression of sexual ecstasy, the music returns to the serenity of the opening and continues through the lava lamp shot.

This parallelism—the music and the intercutting of the silent film with the massage scene—provide more than enough information to draw the inference that Benigno has sexual intercourse with Alicia. As the line of action in the silent movie progresses in a certain direction, this sets up the expectation that Benigno and Alicia's story will develop similarly. But rather than actually show Benigno's entry into Alicia's body, the film offers the lava lamp as a visual metaphor for the merging of bodily fluids in the sexual act itself.

There are two questions to ask about this sequence. First, how does it shape the tenor—both emotional and ethical—of Benigno's sexual act? And second, why is the act itself omitted? The answers to these questions are, I suggest, interrelated.

One effective principle of narration is to omit a pivotal story event from the plot[3] and leave it to the viewer's inference. But there is much more to Almodóvar's omission, for it would be positively gross and brutal to see a man mount an unconscious hospitalized woman, moving about vigorously until he climaxes while she lies lifeless under him.

But wait a minute, you might say. This is *Almodóvar* we're talking about, a filmmaker who revels in, rather than shies away from, the crude and shocking. I take this point, and do not mean to suggest that it's the vulgar or violent nature of such a scene that explains its omission. Rather, I suggest that the lacuna hides from view the repulsiveness of Benigno's actions, thereby making it considerably more difficult to see them—and him—as criminal. Since we do not see the repugnant act itself, we can easily avoid thinking of it as a rape, which is exactly what the sequence I've been discussing encourages us to do.

To see what I mean, let's consider a contrasting case. Early in Quentin Tarantino's *Kill Bill*, the protagonist (played by Uma Thurman) wakes up from a four-year coma.[4] When she hears an orderly enter the room she pretends to be comatose. The orderly, we learn, is prostituting Thurman to a trucker. The orderly gives the trucker a set of instructions that make the viewer aware of the sordid details of this sort of exchange without actually showing them. These instructions indicate just how brutal and nasty things can get: "Rule number one: no punching her. Nurse comes in tomorrow and she got a shiner or less teeth, jig's up. . . . Now, rule number two: no monkey bites, no hickeys. In fact—no leaving no marks of no kind. After that, it's all good, buddy. Her plumbing don't work no more so come in her all you want. Keep the noise down. Try not to make a mess." The orderly starts to leave the room to allow the trucker to "have himself a good time." Before exiting, he remembers something: "Oh! Shit. By the way, sometimes this chick's cooch can get drier than a bucket of sand. If she's dry, just lube up with this and you'll be good to go," and with that he throws the client a noticeably grimy container of petroleum jelly. The trucker then mounts the bed and pushes his face toward the apparently comatose Thurman who lies pale, unwashed and sickly. "Oh, goddamn," he says lasciviously as he pushes his mouth toward her pallid face, "you are the best-looking girl I've had today." She then assaults him and manages to escape.

Up to the point where Thurman assaults the trucker, the contents of Tarantino's and Almodóvar's scenarios are quite similar, yet the moods couldn't be more different. Although Tarantino also does not show the moment of intercourse, the film alludes to the sexual act in all of its sordid and brutal details, offers the gruesome spectacle of a man clumsily mounting the hospital bed of a wan comatose woman and forces us to confront nasty specifics like the matter of lubrication. Tarantino neither sanitizes nor prettifies the event. The woman lies pallid and unwashed in her hospital gown, her oily hair framing her sickly face. Her gauntness and unhealthy complexion are enhanced by the harsh green glow of institutional lighting. There is no music—only the mechanical rhythm of an electrocardiogram.

Almodóvar, by contrast, spares us all of the unpleasant and sordid details, offering instead a warmly lit room, gentle music, and a titillating view of a bare-breasted, beautiful woman who is fully made-up and simply but elegantly dressed. And in place of intercourse we are offered a soothing visual metaphor accompanied by romantic music that encourages us to think of the sexual act as flowing, tranquil, and even beautiful.

The auspicious character of Benigno's sexual act is enhanced by the parallelism with the silent film, which tells the story of a genuine couple in love. This falls right in line with Benigno's misperception of his relationship with Alicia. And although Alfredo's entry into Amparo's vagina counts as rape—for she cannot consent when asleep, and the fact that he is her boyfriend does not entitle him to unlimited access to her body[5]—the silent film does not present it as a violation. Consider, for instance, the light-hearted and even comic tone about Alfredo's climbing onto her mountainous breasts and into her enormous vagina. Further, his diminished size makes him seem hardly threatening and incapable of brutality. And finally, her ecstatic response puts to rest any suspicion we might have of violation; she is obviously enjoying herself.

The silent film sets up the expectation that the situation between Benigno and Alicia will develop in a similar direction. But that's not its only function. "Shrinking Lover" also unabashedly proclaims the acceptability of sexual intercourse with an unconscious woman. Alfredo's entry into Amparo's vagina is portrayed as an act of love from which she derives benefit (in the form of pleasure), rather than a violation, and this tutors us in how to understand Benigno's parallel act. To complete the similarity, there is a strong suggestion (made by Marco) at the end of the film that the rape and subsequent birth actually brought Alicia out of the coma. Her benefit is not sexual pleasure but, rather, a return to conscious life itself, a kind of rebirth, as Robert B. Pippin points out in his essay in this collection.

Taken together, these elements—the omission of the sexual act itself, its replacement by the visual metaphor of the lava lamp and the silent film's portrayal of rape as an act of love—lend Benigno's intercourse with Alicia a consensual, loving, and favorable tone. And this, in conjunction with the three features mentioned earlier—the emphasis on Benigno's devotion and altruism, the film's explicit presentation of them as a couple and Benigno's recognition of Alicia's personhood through talk— indeed give the appearance of a story of true love, not sexual violation. The film shapes our perception of Benigno's act so that it seems beautiful, benevolent, beneficent, and *almost* mutual. It's no wonder, then, that critics repeatedly refer to theirs as a "love story."

Our discussion thus far may incline one to think that *Talk to Her* should simply take its place among the ranks of the many artworks in the western tradition that present a rape as if it were not a rape—from the rapes of Greek and Roman mythology onward.[6] Perhaps *Talk to Her* is just another of those works that tries to convince us, however subtly, that rapists are really good guys after all and that rapes actually benefit women in the long run.

You don't have to be a hardcore feminist to find this all too familiar message unsavory. The problem is this: rape and the constant threat of rape play a significant role in women's subordination[7] and our society continues to deal with this inadequately; our legal system fails to properly punish the crime and our culture does little to discourage it.[8] Indeed, many forms of culture—from high art to popular culture, from the ancient to the modern—encourage rape, or at the very least apologize for it.[9] Such encouragements and apologies coming from both high and popular culture are part of what sustains and promotes gender inequality. *Talk to Her* is one such work insofar as it romanticizes rape, downplays its harms, ascribes to it imaginary benefits, and encourages sympathy for its perpetrators. The film is ethically defective, then, insofar as it calls upon viewers to adopt attitudes toward rape that play a role in the reproduction of gender inequality. This is not a peripheral or otherwise insignificant dimension of the film but, rather, lies at the center of its drama.

Yet, as the ballet mistress explicitly reminds us near the film's end, "nothing is simple." *Talk to Her* is not just another work that denies rape—and in this way it is unlike "Shrinking Lover"—for, as I have mentioned, the viewer is primed early on to think of Benigno as failing to respect Alicia's personal boundaries. Indeed, the scene where he intrudes into her room makes him appear psychopathic and stalkerish, preparing us to think of him as a violator. More important, all the aestheticization in the world couldn't completely remove one's sense that there is something deeply wrong with having intercourse with a comatose woman, no matter how much one loves her. When the judgment of rape comes at the end of the film, it seems entirely appropriate. There's no suggestion that Benigno's colleagues and friends shouldn't be appalled, and his punishment is presented as just.

What I mean to suggest is that *Talk to Her* falls somewhere between *Shrinking Lover* and *Kill Bill* in its attitude toward rape. On the one hand, it aestheticizes and sanitizes the rape to the point that it almost doesn't seem like a rape, yet on the other hand it gives us just enough to forestall this conclusion.

This is to say that Almodóvar is walking a fine line, portraying one and the same act as a rape and a not-rape, and one and the same actor as a rapist and a benevolent caretaker. This is a delicate balance to maintain: foregrounding the non-consensual intercourse (for instance by representing the event itself) would render Benigno too monstrous and vicious for us to feel sympathy and compassion for him. But if the film completely sanitized and prettified the rape, then it would no longer appear to be a crime, Benigno would seem a mere victim of unfair charges, and we would feel unconflicted outrage at his downfall. Either way, the film would be considerably less compelling, a point to which I return shortly. Almodóvar delicately navigates these two poles, forcing us to confront Benigno's crime while simultaneously demanding our pity and compassion for his loss of the beloved.

I say "demand" because the film works extremely hard to cultivate our sympathy and compassion for Benigno. It's not just that he presents a benevolent, altruistic and caring persona through most of the film; he is also the pathetic victim of an abusive childhood, having been forced to devote most of his life to inappropriately intimate care for his mother. He has never had any friends or lovers and is so piteous that he doesn't even realize that his childhood was stolen from him. With respect to Alicia's rape, one almost wants to say that Benigno doesn't know any better, except—and this is part of Almodóvar's brilliance—that he clearly *does*. In these and other ways, the film cultivates our sympathy, pity, and compassion for Benigno. We pity him for being imprisoned, not so much because he's being punished but because of the painful separation from his beloved, the only one he's ever had. As he puts it in his suicide note to Marco, he cannot bear to live in a world without so much as Alicia's hairclip. This sentimental expression pulls our heart strings in favor of Benigno, but it does so over a piece of property that was not come by honestly; the hairclip, we remember, was *stolen* when Benigno stalked Alicia and intruded into her bedroom. Even in the sentimental moments, Almodóvar reminds us of Benigno's dark side.

And herein lies my struggle with the film, for it enjoins us to respond in ways that we oughtn't, where the force of the "oughtn't" is ethical. The business with the hairclip is a good example: the film demands our compassion for a man who laments his loss of dominion over an unconscious woman. My ethical commitments counsel me to celebrate this loss, not lament it with him. Likewise with Alicia's rape: in the ways described above, the film fashions her sexual violation as beautiful, beneficent, mutual, and even erotic, but these are not appropriate attitudes to take toward an act of subordination and degradation, even if it is only a fictional one. These two things go hand in hand, as I've mentioned, since our sympathy for Benigno depends upon our interpreting the rape as something other than a rape; although we are supposed to see Benigno's actions as wrong, "rape" seems a far too sordid and vicious term to apply in this case. In order to do these things—that is, in order to see Benigno and Alicia as a couple; to see his intercourse with her as romantic, beneficial, and beautiful; to feel compassion and tender sorrow for the distress that Benigno has brought upon himself by taking sexual advantage of an utterly helpless woman—I must, to use a Humean locution, pervert the sentiments of my heart.[10] That is, the film asks us to see its world in light of a pernicious set of evaluative concepts, and this we have good reason to avoid on ethical grounds.

In this way, Almodóvar's film is ethically defective. But what do such defects mean for our overall evaluation of the film as a work of art? Hume urges that such ethical flaws actually mar the artistic character of a work:

> Where vicious manners are described, without being marked with the proper characters of blame and disapprobation; this must be allowed to disfigure the [work], and to be a real deformity. I cannot, nor is it proper that I should, enter into such sentiments; and however I may excuse the [author], on account of the manners of his age, I can never relish the composition.[11]

Why should Hume say that an ethical defect counts as a real "deformity" (which in his terminology is the contrary of beauty) and that he can never relish such a work's "composition?" Why should a work's unethical character diminish its aesthetic quality? Hume provides only a hint of an explanation, but a recent movement in the philosophy of art that I shall call *ethicism* has filled out the Humean position and provided it with arguments.[12] Ethicism holds that in certain cases a work's ethical flaws can diminish its artistic value and that its ethical merits can augment its artistic value.

Here is the general shape of the most convincing argument for ethicism, which was developed by Noël Carroll and Berys Gaut.[13] Artworks, especially representational ones, often solicit attitudes from their audience. Let us call the sum of these solicitations a work's *agenda*.

Failure to engender an attitude that is part of a work's agenda is an artistic defect: it is the defect of being unsuccessful at provoking a response that the work aims to provoke. So, for instance, the thriller that does not provoke a sudden and sharp feeling of excitement is to this extent artistically defective, and defective on its own terms—that is, the terms being set out by the work's agenda. Now, some attitudes that a work solicits are unwarranted in the sense that there is good ethical reason not to feel them. For instance, we have ethical reasons to reject racial stereotypes or homophobic sentiments, and any work that solicits such attitudes is to that extent ethically flawed. But such a work is also *artistically* flawed, according to ethicism, in that it solicits a response that we ought not to have, or, to put it another way, such a work gives us good reason not to respond in a way required for its own artistic success. And, as mentioned at the start of this paragraph, this is one kind of artistic defect: being unsuccessful at provoking the attitude that the work aims to provoke.

At its best, ethicism is a cautious and moderate view. First, it holds not that ethical features of a work trump all other considerations when assessing the work's overall artistic value, but rather that this influence of the ethical flaw upon a work's overall artistic merit admits of *degrees*. A work's various defects and merits must be weighed against one another in an all-things-considered judgment of the work's overall value.[14] Second, ethicism does not hold that *every* ethical defect of the sort described above will be artistically relevant, since some ethical flaws might be downright peripheral to the work's overall aims and thus utterly outweighed by meritorious features that remain untouched by the defect.[15] Finally, ethicism is responsive to degrees of severity in ethical defect when balancing and weighing a work's virtues and vices.[16] Romanticizing shoplifting, say, is a much less serious ethical flaw than romanticizing rape, and the former, even when central to a work's agenda, should diminish a work considerably less than the latter. In sum, at its best ethicism avoids the pronouncement of global ethical standards for artistic relevance, holding instead that an ethical flaw in an artwork can sometimes diminish, but not necessarily destroy, the work's artistic value.

Ethicism offers a powerful argument for a longstanding intuition, dating back far beyond Hume to Plato and Aristotle, that moral and artistic value do not exist separately in airtight compartments but, rather, can impinge upon one another. But exactly how the artistic and the ethical impinge upon one another is a matter of debate and ethicism faces some serious challenges on just this point.[17] One thing ethicism cannot explain is why the influence of the ethical upon the artistic should be asymmetrical. Why should ethical defects sometimes yield artistic defects yet not also sometimes yield artistic merits? And why shouldn't ethical merits sometimes yield artistic defects?

It's not so difficult to see why the latter might be true, for many works suffer artistically precisely because they are morally praiseworthy. Moral virtues can yield a host of artistic failings, including making a work preachy (Jenny Holzer), pat (Charles Dickens), sentimental (Norman Rockwell), or flat-out boring. Examples of works that are bad (artistically speaking) precisely because they are good (ethically speaking) abound, although ethicists do not attend to them. But it appears more difficult to come up with examples of the works that are artistically enhanced by their ethical flaws.[18] Indeed, philosophical discussion on the topic has yet to produce any convincing examples. So I'd like to offer *Talk to Her* as an example of *immoralism*: the view that ethical flaws in an artwork can yield artistic merits. I contend that *Talk to Her* achieves its artistic excellence largely *because* of its ethical flaws, not *despite* them.

Talk to Her is just the kind of work that should cause an ethicist to pause on this score, for if the movie is artistically good—and I agree with the critics that it is very good—it achieves this excellence precisely because it is unethical in the way that ethicism describes. That is, the film is good because it succeeds in provoking responses that we have good ethical reason to resist.

As mentioned earlier, the film is not *entirely* depraved. It gives us just enough to judge Benigno appropriately and condemn his crime rather than excuse it. We are not supposed to consider him to have acted rightly. If you disagree, imagine a depraved viewer who found the idea of intercourse with a comatose woman to be romantic and sexy and who believed that Benigno's actions were not just permissible but laudable because of their salutary effects. Such a person wouldn't "get" the movie at all because he wouldn't feel the dilemma that the film sets for us: namely, feeling torn between feelings of sympathy and antipathy, attraction and disgust, praise and blame. Our imagined depraved viewer would miss all of this and would instead feel outrage at Benigno's punishment.

It's not simply that the film palpably sets us a persistent and gripping dilemma that makes it so good, but that it *succeeds* in making us feel things that we oughtn't. It's wrong, for reasons I described earlier, to see a rape as romantic, erotic, and beneficial to its victim, just as it's wrong to pity a rapist for no longer having access to his victim. And yet we do see the erotic beauty and the benefit of Benigno's crime and we do suffer with him for his loss. It is this capacity to manipulate us and make us feel things against our better judgment that makes this film so compelling.

If you think that I'm wrong about this, imagine that the film were not unethical in the way that I've described. This need not take the form of an overt moral tag, as Hume suggests. Instead, imagine that the film did not enjoin us to think of Benigno and Alicia as a couple, did not so strongly solicit compassion for him, and represented his rape of Alicia as a rape in at least some of its gruesome detail (à la Tarantino). Ethically sanitizing the film in this way would not only *not* enhance it artistically, but also wouldn't even leave its most redeeming artistic qualities intact. If Benigno were presented as all bad and his actions as entirely gruesome and deplorable, there would be no dilemma nor any unsettling manipulation of our feelings. Nothing but a simple morality tale would remain and although this might satisfy us morally, it would leave us cold and unmoved.

That is, what's good about *Talk to Her* is that it succeeds in eliciting responses that our ethical commitments counsel us to resist. If we do, for this reason, engage in what Richard Moran calls "imaginative resistance" and refuse to adopt the attitudes that the film solicits, then we just won't get what's compelling about the film.[19] For my part anyway, such resistance is futile, for once exposed to the film I can't help but see Benigno in a sympathetic light and can't avoid acknowledging the felicitous affects of his actions. The film makes me feel and imagine what I deem it wrong to feel and imagine, and in this way it divides me against myself. That it leaves me torn and unsettled is precisely what makes the film unforgettable.

My suggestion, then, is that *Talk to Her* is an excellent case of an ethical defect yielding artistic merits. The film is good (artistically) precisely because it is bad (ethically). Although this does not mean that we should return to segregating the ethical and artistic value of a work into discrete compartments, it does give us reason to rethink the conclusions of ethicism.

Notes

1 Here are just a few examples: writing for The New Yorker, David Denby notes that "both love affairs are touched by fantasy. Almodóvar's point appears to be that you can't have love without fable—that every love affair is an improbable narrative wrung from non-being and loneliness" ("Obsessions," The New Yorker, November 25, 2002, available from The New Yorker Film File). Roger Ebert writes: "conventional morality requires us to disapprove of actions that in fact may have been inspired by love and hope" (Chicago Sun-Times, December 25, 2002). Moira Macdonald finishes her review by noting that the film is "ultimately a tribute to the balm that words provide, and to the infinite variations of love" (The Seattle Times, December 25, 2002).

2 Carrie Rickey, "Two Men Get Lost In Love," Philadelphia Inquirer, December 25, 2002.

3 "Plot" here refers to everything visibly and audibly present in the film before us.

4 Scene 7 on the DVD, minutes 27:30—29:25.

5 When I presented this paper at the Central Division Meetings of the American Philosophical Association, a member of the audience objected that Alfredo's actions could not have counted as rape because he and Amparo were a bona fide couple. There are two things to say in response. First, being in a couple does not give a man unlimited license to his partner's body. Even when in a relationship, a woman is entitled to decline sexual intercourse and if the man persists then this counts as rape. It has been a recent advance of rape law, for instance, that it is now generally recognized that a husband can rape his wife. Second, if Alfredo had Amparo's consent to enter her vagina, why did he wait until she was asleep to do it? The fact that he did not do it while she was conscious suggests that he knew full well that he did not have her consent.

6 For an enlightening treatment of the art historical tradition, see Wolfthal (1999). For a philosophical discussion of one famous work by Titian, see Eaton (2003).

7 Brownmiller (1975) provided the first thorough and eloquent explanation of rape's function as a means to keep women in a state of fear and thereby perpetuate male dominance. For more recent accounts of rape as a technique for maintaining gender inequality, see Stock (1991) and MacKinnon (1989, chapter 9; 2001, chapter 7.1).

8 On the failings of our current legal system to deal properly with rape, see Estrich (1987) and Taslitz (1999). Taslitz also makes the convincing case that cultural narratives (such as novels, films, television, and popular music) have significant and detrimental influence on how rape cases are perceived and dealt with in court.

9 For examples see essays in Tomaselli and Porter (1986), Higgins and Silver (1991), and Eaton (2003).

10 Hume (1985).

11 p. 246.

12 The term was coined by Berys Gaut in his 1997 essay, although the view is held under different names and elaborated by many, especially by Noël Carroll (1996 and 2000).

13 First developed in Gaut's 1997 essay and further refined in his 2001 essay.

14 Berys Gaut insists on this (Gaut: 2001, p. 347).

15 The idea that ethical defects are only *sometimes* artistically relevant is the cornerstone of Noël Carroll's moderate moralism. See Carroll (1996 and 2000, pp. 377 ff.).

16 I make this point (Eaton: 2003, p. 176), and offer an example from Italian Renaissance painting.

17 Daniel Jacobson offers the most trenchant and thorough criticism of ethicism. See Jacobson 1997 and 2006.

18 Noël Carroll appears to allow that moderate moralism (his version of what I'm calling ethicism) is not committed to denying that moral defects can at times make an artistic contribution to a work but, he says, "few, if any, examples come to mind" (Carroll: 2000, p. 380). Jacobson offers three examples in his 1997 essay but none of these are convincing, as Carroll himself demonstrates (Carroll: 2000, p. 380, n. 34).

19 See Moran (1994).

Works cited

Brownmiller, Susan. 1975. *Against Our Will: Men, Women, and Rape.* New York: Fawcett Columbine.

Carroll, Noël. 1996. "Moderate Moralism." In *British Journal of Aesthetics* 36 (3): 223–38.

——. 2000. "Art and Ethical Criticism." In *Ethics* 110 (January 2000): 350–87.

Eaton, A.W. "Where Ethics and Aesthetics Meet." In *Hypatia: A Journal of Feminist Philosophy* (Winter 2003).

Estrich, S. 1987. *Real Rape.* Cambridge, MA: Harvard University Press.

Gaut, B. 1997. "The Ethical Criticism of Art." In Jerrold Levinson (ed.), *Aesthetics and Ethics.* Cambridge: Cambridge University Press.

——. 2001. "Art and Ethics." In B. Gaut and D. Lopes (eds), *The Routledge Companion to Aesthetics.* London: Routledge, pp. 341–52.

Higgins, L. and B. Silver (eds). 1991. *Rape and Representation.* New York: Columbia University Press.

Hume, David. 1985. "Of the Standard of Taste." In Eugene F. Miller (ed.), *Essays: Moral, Political, and Literary.* Indianapolis: Liberty Fund, pp. 226–49.

Jacobson, Daniel. 1997. "In Praise of Immoral Art." In *Philosophical Topics* 25: 155–99.

——. 2006. "Ethical Criticism and the Vice of Moderation." In Matthew Kieran (ed.), *Contemporary Debates in Aesthetics and the Philosophy of Art.* Blackwell Publishers.

MacKinnon, Catharine A. 1989. *Toward a Feminist Theory of the State.* Harvard University Press.

——. 2001. *Sex Equality* (University Casebook Series). Foundation Press.

Moran, R. 1994. "The Expression of Feeling in Imagination." In *The Philosophical Review* 103: 75–106.

Stock, Wendy E. 1991. "Feminist Explanations: Male Power, Hostility, and Sexual Coercion." In E. Grauerholz and M. Koralewski (eds), *Sexual Coercion: A Sourcebook on its Nature, Causes, and Prevention.* Lexington, MA: Lexington Books, pp. 61–73.

Taslitz, A. 1999. *Rape and the Culture of the Courtroom.* New York: New York University Press.

Tomaselli, S. and R. Porter (eds). 1986. *Rape: a Historical and Social Enquiry.* Oxford: Basil Blackwell Ltd.

Wolfthal, Diane. 1999. *Images of Rape: the "Heroic" Tradition and its Alternatives.* Cambridge: Cambridge University Press.

Chapter 3

Robert B. Pippin

DEVILS AND ANGELS IN
ALMODÓVAR'S *TALK TO HER*

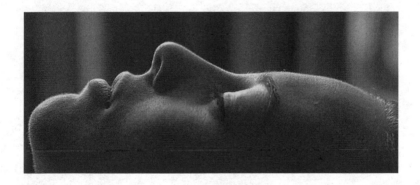

S TANLEY CAVELL HAS WRITTEN THAT THE "dramatic mode of film is the mythological" and that this mythical dimension is actually "the typical."[1] There would seem to be little typical about a world of comatose women, a barely sane, largely delusional male nurse, a woman bullfighter, and a rape that leads to a "rebirth" in a number of senses. But comatose women, the central figures in Almodóvar's *Talk to Her*, are, oddly, very familiar in that mythological genre closest to us: fairy tales. Both Snow White and Sleeping Beauty are comatose women who endure—"non-consensually" we must say—a male kiss, male sexual attention. (Siegfried's awakening kiss of Brunnhilde in the extraordinary third act of *Siegfried* should also be mentioned.)[2] Someone apparently must manifest some act of faith, must believe that these corpse-like women are not dead, and believe it strongly enough to kiss them. Then there is a kind of inversion of these fairy tales in Kleist's story and Roehmer's film, *Die Marquise von O.* Here the kiss is actually a rape, but the rapist again emerges as some sort of Prince Charming after all (he had originally saved the Marquise from rape by a group of Russian soldiers), and there are echoes of that somewhat disturbing notion of reconciliation as well in the Almodóvar film. (Alicia, after all, does awaken.) In the Kleist story, a woman must place an ad in a newspaper asking her unknown rapist (she was drugged and asleep) and the father of her unborn child to come forward. He does eventually and the story ends with their marriage and with one of the most enigmatic lines in all of literature, as enigmatic, I think, as our complex reactions to Benigno's act: the Marquise says that she would not have thought her new husband a devil if he had not first appeared as an angel, as if one person *can* be both devil and angel, that, to the extent that one can be an angel, to *that* extent he also can be a devil.

We do not seem to recoil morally in the fairy tale cases, as if the sleeping beauties were victims of unwanted male attention, as if yet more examples of male fantasies of passive, wholly dependent women whose very waking lives depend utterly on bold sexual attention by men, regardless of considerations of equity or consent. This is probably because the narrative frame of the fairy tales suggests that such a moment is fated; it *must* happen, these princes are for these women and them alone. The kiss is also more like medical attention to accident victims; the princes can't just leave the beauties sleeping there and we presumably are meant to think that Prince Charmings are universal types; that they would, by definition, be the object choice of any woman once awakened; and, given the fate theme, especially be the object choice of these princesses.

We *do* recoil, however, at Benigno; it is simply horrific imagining him on top of the nearly lifeless, unmoving body of Alicia. We also have a very different reaction on a second viewing. Once we know what Benigno will do, what we had first taken to be his tender medical ministrations now look suspicious. He is occasionally all too casual about Alicia's nudity; his complimentary remarks about Alicia's breasts might have rushed past on first viewing. They don't on a subsequent viewing, once we know where his attention is leading. But still, all in all, I think it is fair to say that we also hesitate to place this rape in exactly the same category as the brutal attempted rape of Uma Thurman's comatose character at the beginning of Kill Bill 1, or Terence Stamp's imprisonment of Samantha Eggar in William Wyler's The Collector (or I think we should, at the very least, hesitate). That very hesitation, or what appears to be something like a sympathetic treatment of Benigno by Almodóvar, is just what can generate a certain unease among some viewers.

There are several obvious elements to this hesitation, to the indeterminacy and unsettledness of our moral response to the character and the act (something ultimately essential to this being an aesthetic treatment, not an example of, or illustrative of, a moral theory). Part of it (hesitating about equating as instances of a kind Benigno and Uma Thurman's attacker) has to do with the fact that the fairy tale context just suggested is close to the fantasy world occupied by Benigno. His act of faith (as he sees it), of keeping faith with Alicia as still a responsive, communicative subject, is for most of the film more delusional than heroic and often simply pathetic. For one thing, Benigno is presented as a figure of desperate loneliness (as is Marco, in a different way), a man who for twenty years lived in a situation crazy enough to drive him slightly mad himself, living only for his mother, attending her, we come to learn, with virtually the same intimacy and diligence required for Alicia, although, bizarrely, the mother was not an invalid but just, according to Benigno, "lazy."[3] And Benigno clearly imagines that he and Alicia have a deep bond because of this, that she is not so much in a "persistent vegetative state," as she is simply someone as alone as he is, that the world he lives in is almost as dark and impenetrable as hers.

Benigno's own view of the rape (figured for us by a very strange silent film he is recounting to Alicia on the night of the rape and which portrays what he is about to do as a return to the womb) is in keeping with this presentation of his mental state as delusional, something that would obviously qualify any moral condemnation. But Benigno's psychopathology only explains part of our hesitation, a hesitation I would describe not as an unwillingness to apply the category of rape, or as a wish to excuse what Benigno did. It rather seems a hesitation simply to leave the matter there, a hesitation about the adequacy of a moral response tout court, and so a way of raising the question of this sort of "qualification" of a moral response; that is, what sort of qualification is

it? Or, what would it mean to concede the authority of the moral point
of view, but deny it the sort of absolute trumping power that, for many,
comes with such authority? The most interesting dimension raised by
the film is just this: *how* does a moral judgment lie alongside of, become
imbricated in (or not), color or shadow, all the other reactions,
projections, and anxieties involved in living a life and in responding to
another? (This is, of course, the most interesting theme of many film
noirs: something that Almodóvar is quite aware of. At the end of *Bad
Education*—a much more noirish film than *Talk to Her*—Juan and Berenguer
go to a film noir festival while the deadly heroin they have given Ignacio
does its work. As they emerge Berenguer (the pederast priest) says,
"Those movies all seemed to be about us.")

Moral philosophers sometimes distinguish between so-called "first-
order" moral judgments—in this case the judgment that what Benigno
did was rape and was wrong—and "second-order" judgments—in this
case whether or to what degree to blame Benigno, to hold him to account
—and they argue that the former judgment can be made without requiring the latter. They also sometimes distinguish between the act itself and
its consequences, and in this case that might lead one to say that whatever
Benigno had intended by having sex with Alicia (and it is very difficult
to infer what exactly he thought he was trying to do or bring about),
her recovery cannot be credited to him.[4] In both cases, especially the former, Benigno's delusory state seems somehow to be both exculpatory
and to block an attribution of Alicia's recovery to his actions.

I don't wish to dispute any of this, but I don't think our "hesitation,"
as I have called it, is based on an appreciation of Benigno's psychopathology. As noted, there is a mythic dimension to the film as well, and
in that dimension Benigno's actions are in a certain way affirmed more
directly, rather than excused, even though the act is morally heinous.
The way this all works in the film is by constant and explicit contrast
with the very "secular," fantasy-less Marco–Lydia parallel plot, and by
its (the film's) indubitable affirmation of Benigno's point of view
with regard to the "talk to her" advice that gives the movie its title. This
highly paradoxical attitude embodied in the film gives it its power and
much of its mystery. The rather conflicted state one is in at the end of
the movie recalls Nietzsche's claim in his *Genealogy of Morals* that it is a sign
of a "higher nature," or a more "spiritual nature," to be able to endure

great "divisions" in the soul, to be a "battleground" of incompatible commitments (I, 16).

We might also note here that Almodóvar's films very often anticipate, solicit, direct, and then up-end or undermine expected audience reactions —including, but not exclusively limited to, moral reactions—as a matter of course. In almost everything he has done, Almodóvar clearly tries to present such issues in ways that will effect a kind of "double shock." The first shock is the oddness of the variation on the typical itself: nuns who take heroin and psychedelic drugs (*Dark Habits*); a mother who sells a child to a pederast (*What Have I Done To Deserve This?*); kidnap victims who fall for their kidnappers (*Tie Me Up! Tie Me Down!*); a pregnant, AIDS-infected nun, and a search for a father and husband who turns out to have become a woman (*All About My Mother*). In *Woman on the Verge of a Nervous Breakdown*, a soap powder commercial presents the mother of a serial killer bragging that she can get her son's clothes so white, so free of blood stains, that it even confounds the forensic police. There are pederast priests (*Bad Education*), and of course the rape of a comatose woman in *Talk to Her*. But the second additional turn of the screw is as interesting and as unusual, for all such cases are not presented as if an invitation to a kind of prurient realism, but clearly with an eye towards some redemptive humanism, some deflection of the discomfort we feel, for example, at obsessive, often nearly insane love (as in the French l'*amour fou* tradition, or the love affair in *Live Flesh*), so that a moment of affirmation is also, quite unexpectedly, possible. In all such cases, while we seem first invited to respond within the conventions of comedy, as if slightly superior to the drag queen camp characters with whom Almodóvar populates his films, there is always also some reversal in which something like the inner strength or reserves of moral courage or great loyalty or generosity are manifested, the dedication and sacrifice of characters we might be tempted to mock or treat simply as "exhibitions."

In fact, there is also a great emphasis on the complexities of exhibition, on gesture, dress, costume, and display, and we are invited to read these signs and gestures conventionally at first, in order to demonstrate subsequently that they are elements of a much more complex drama in which the interpretative work is much more difficult, the results much less determinate. The difficulty of knowing who anybody actually is or what part they are playing, in whose narration, from what point of view, reaches a kind of apotheosis in *Bad Education*, which features a plot in which a character has written a story about a person who was abused by a priest, became a transvestite and wrote a story about the abuse, with which he is trying to blackmail the priest, and the author in the story is supposed to be author of the story, the character we see on screen originally. Except that character is not the character of the story and the story within the story. It is actually his brother, who has murdered his transgendered brother (the real author), and is pretending to be the real character. This "point-of-view uncertainty" is often invoked in Almodóvar's films as a way of reminding us how little we know about the characters who we are tempted to judge conventionally and often morally. So in Talk to Her everyone, especially Alicia's father, thinks they know that an effeminate male nurse just has to be gay, and everyone is obsessed with the heterosexual affairs of a female bullfighter, as if her femaleness in itself were hard to believe.

Another qualification or reason to hesitate in our judgment is purely aesthetic. The Pina Bausch dance, Café Müller, that begins the movie is clearly a kind of allegory of the film, a way of letting us know that the narrative frame of the story is certainly not "realistic" in the conventional or theatrical sense, that the action we are about to see has much more the logic of a dream (or a myth) than a standard plot.[5] The silent movie at the center of things, The Shrinking Lover, makes this "irrealizing" point again and I will return to both the silent dance and the silent movie later. That is, Benigno's fantasy is as strange and crazy as the silent movie, and the film we are watching is more like an expressivist silent film or an avant garde dance than a straight melodrama.[6] But for now we can appreciate that such an unusual way of framing what we are about to see also makes a straightforward moral reaction as incomplete and inade-quate as would be the judgment that the Lisa Berndle character in Max Ophüls's Letter from an Unknown Woman is a deluded crackpot who foolishly throws her own life away and those of her son and husband and even her great beloved; or as inadequate, say, as the final judgment that Medea was a "bad person" for having killed her children.

The judgment about Benigno also appears qualified "inside" the film by the fact that the far more realistic and sober "scientific" assessments of Lydia's comatose condition by Marco and Lydia's former boyfriend ("The Valencia Kid") seem somehow connected with Lydia's death; and it is all even more qualified by Alicia's rebirth: her return to consciousness and eventual mobility and possible life. Marco quite properly points out at one point that what Benigno is doing is indistinguishable from "talking to plants," but within the narrative frame created by the movie Alicia clearly seems brought back to life by what Benigno does, even though what he does clearly calls for some moral recoil. There is also an echo of the Bausch dance that is relevant to this issue in the horrific scene of Lydia being gored by the bull, and not just because Rosario Flores is so extraordinarily balletic. On the one hand what Lydia is doing is very foolhardy. She opens with a kind of pass, a *porta gayola*, that is usually only attempted at the very end of a *corrida* when the bull is very tired and weak.[7] (She is on her knees, with her cape in front of her, and expects to make a pass just by shifting her body, not her feet.) But this pose dramatizes something we can already sense from implied comparison with the dance choreography: she has no help, as Alicia does (now or in her coma), no one to "clear the chairs away," and that is the way she wants it; she is facing this huge animal, this agent of death, on her own, as if supremely self-sufficient.[8] In fact, in this magnificent scene the expression on Lydia's face suggests such defiance and hubris, such a "silent" but eloquent challenge to what seems to be the embodiment of male power, perhaps even male sexuality, in this huge bull, that we fear some line has been crossed, that she is infinitely admirable for this expression of will, but, we know, doomed. There is also something mythologically significant in the fact that both these utterly passive, inaccessible women are rendered comatose violently, forced into a state that is sometimes intimated as a figure for the "forced" role of the feminine itself, at least by Benigno, in that chilling scene where he treats talking to Alicia as an instance of the general advice one ought to follow with regard to all women—talk to them, take them seriously—as if this might not occur to us without a reminder; as if the default position of most men is to act as if women were comatose. But that is an independent topic.

Of course, all these sorts of questions can only arise if we assume that we can attribute intentional states, even moral attitudes to the work itself, and that prompts some very familiar issues in aesthetics. But for purposes of this discussion, I think we should just agree at the outset that Benigno and his act *are* partly treated sympathetically by Almodóvar. For one thing, Benigno is allowed to present most of the movie's details to us, and this point of view is only directly challenged by Marco, who is clearly sympathetic, and this only occasionally. The last thing Benigno has done (within, let us say, the frame of relevance, salience and moral import created by Almodóvar and Benigno) is to treat Alicia merely as an object, a thing to be used for his pleasure. Indeed, Almodóvar spends a great deal of camera time detailing the quite involved ministrations of Benigno and his fellow nurses (Rosa and Mathilde) for Alicia, clearly treating the ablutions and dressing as ritualistic in a religious sense, all in a way parallel with the long beautiful scene of Lydia (whose name means "bull-fighting")[9] being dressed for the bullfight. (Compare with the undressing of Father Manolo's vestments in Bad Education.) Benigno's care for Alicia is clearly meant to be enveloping and tender (although for the most part only from his point of view, and even though we slowly begin to see that there is something dangerously obsessive and possessive in his treatment). Even (and here again our unease) the sexual assault cannot fully be understood except within such a context. And everything he does also seems continuous with the insistent humanism (the insistent refusal to allow her to slip into the status of mere objecthood) embodied in his "talk to her" advice to Marco, the journalist with whom he forms a deep bond of friendship. (Personhood, the film almost suggests, depends on the kind of affirmation and faith exhibited by Benigno; it is a status achieved only by virtue of such reciprocal affirmations and is not a matter of fact property of some animals.) It is this sympathy (essentially Marco's sympathy, a reaction not unconnected with his own failings) and the hesitation it provokes that we must understand.

Indeed, in many ways the movie is mostly about this growing, awkward friendship between the two men, not so much about the two women and their fate.[10] It is Alicia's comatose body that initially connects them and this link is the pivot on which our ultimate reaction to the film will turn. Marco walks by Alicia's room once when she is naked and being attended to. Benigno invites him in, and Marco is clearly extremely uncomfortable in the room with Alicia's body (which, incredibly, remains a beautiful body) so visible. We are not really sure if he is uncomfortable because he feels sexually excited by the sight and is confused by and embarrassed by this response, or because he is quite understandably puzzled that Benigno could treat Alicia's need for privacy so cavalierly, exposing her so calmly to strangers. Likewise it allows a measure of doubt about Benigno to enter the viewer's mind; we are not sure if this exposure is just part of the infamous depersonalization and lack of privacy endemic to hospital culture, or if this is a sign that Benigno's proprietary sense of his control of Alicia is already somewhat out of hand. (This dialectical relation between respectful subservience and nursing as a form of control will emerge again later.)

Later, in the crucial "talk to her" scene at the heart of the film, this same uncertainty about Alicia's nakedness happens again, but the viewer now seems to be led away from some of these doubts and towards Benigno's point of view. Marco remarks to Benigno that he could never touch and move Lydia in the way Benigno ministers to Alicia, that he is somewhat repelled by her barely alive physical form. Right before this conversation, he had learned that his position as principal lover and chief mourner had all been an illusion, that Lydia had turned back to Niño even before the bullfighting accident, and so, with the best will in the world, he had "read" everything wrong; that there was something almost as comical in his position as the *rejected* lover, dutifully attending a woman in love with someone else, as there is in Benigno thinking he will marry Alicia. Even with both women in comas, the various love triangles continue to be upset and to reform. After Marco's remark about his distaste for Lydia's body and Benigno's advice—"talk to her, tell her that," as if he is encouraging something like couple's counseling—we also see from this moment on that Marco accepts at least some aspects of Benigno's point of view (perhaps because he realizes that an important aspect of his own reasonable, prudent view had itself been a great illusion); accepts that however deluded and morally inappropriate, there is something in Benigno's relation to Alicia (his keeping faith, his refusal to allow her any object status) that moral and even scientific categories alone will not capture.

This is so to such an extent that by the end of the film, Marco comes more and more to re-occupy Benigno's life, his place in the world, and that is yet another factor in our hesitation (as instructed by the logic of the film) to condemn Benigno—this fact that we begin to see him through Marco's eyes. He lives in Benigno's apartment after the latter's suicide, re-occupies Benigno's "view" of the dance studio, and begins even to live out Benigno's deepest fantasy by beginning what we are clearly meant to think is the start of a relationship with the now recovering Alicia. And most of all, despite his earlier insistence that talking to the comatose Alicia was like talking to plants, Marco himself begins to talk to the corpse of Benigno in Benigno's grave. This all suggests that Marco has learned something from Benigno's craziness, so much so that the characters even seem to merge.[11]

This happens visually. There is a Bergman-esque, or *Persona*-like scene at the end when Benigno is in prison that makes this point extremely well. Almodóvar has set up the shot so that the reflections of each man superimpose on each other in the glass partitions; they merge with each other. The scene also establishes that Benigno's environment now perfectly mirrors the profound isolation of his life: in a glass cage, able to see others but almost as cut off from them as his beloved Alicia. The contrast with the central "talk to her" scene will also establish what an extraordinary acting job is done by Javier Camera as Benigno. His character changes very dramatically after the exposure of what he has done (or, one could say, after he knows he will get caught). The sweetness and gentleness of the nurse are replaced by a kind of grim determination; the effeminate features, the graceful, confident gestures, are all gone; and an almost violent, barely suppressed rage can be detected, all as if to try to suggest again that these two opposed elements can coexist, even as the monstrosity of Benigno's violation can at the same time be an act of faith and affirmation, that it being the former does not exclude it being the latter. The echo of Kleist's devil–angel dyad and the familiar moral complexities of film noir are again relevant. (One should note also that the transformation is disturbing too. It faintly suggests that Benigno might have been originally acting out a part, playing himself as an idealized type ("caring and innocent nurse"), and that what we see now is not a new role, but the unadorned Benigno. Whether this changes what I have been calling our "moral hesitation" is quite a complicated issue, as complicated as the question of the difference between being who one is and "playing at being who one is.")

At any rate, Marco's reaction to the new Benigno, beginning when Benigno tells him that he wants to marry Alicia, indicates that Marco realizes he had been treating Benigno's obsession in too mediated, symbolic or expressivist a way, that he had not realized how deadly serious Benigno was about Alicia. And since both Marco and Benigno's co-worker, Rosa, express what Almodóvar clearly takes to be the standard, reasonable, initially sympathetic audience reaction (the nurse says on the phone to Marco: "He (Benigno) has done a monstrous thing, but that doesn't mean he shouldn't be helped"), we also feel somewhat shocked, perhaps guilty in having believed in Benigno's harmlessness; perhaps engaged too much with the literary and figurative and fantastical dimensions of the actual plot, we might say. We also clearly feel what

Marco and Rosa feel: the pull of loyalty to a character in the way in which we might feel such a pull for a brother or sister or child who had done something horrible, where such an act, while a reason to condemn, is not a reason to abandon.

But still, in many ways *Talk to Her*, by making use of rape, takes the greatest risks with viewer reaction and an obvious question is whether this can be said to work. (There is a much more complicated dimension to this question of the aesthetic success: the fact that for all the pathos and melodrama and even horror, the movie also works as a comedy: a much longer issue.) In *Talk to Her*, we might say, whether it all "works" or not comes down to an interpretation both of how to characterize the rape—as a straightforward abuse of intimacy and power by a self-absorbed neurotic, or as (at least from Benigno's point of view) a genuine act of love, even sacrifice (as it turns out); or as a mere case history, the pathological acts of a deluded ill man; or as a quasi-mythic re-enactment of a male fantasy about female dependence or male power. The question of what it means that Benigno's rape is somehow—and it is not at all clear how—tied to Alicia's recovery requires some decision about these alternatives, or about how to think all of them together, if they are in some sense all true, as they probably are. Put another way, the movie will sound the right tone, will end up, let us say, credible, if the clear link between Benigno's monomaniacal, even psychopathological dedication to Alicia could *also* seem a version of love, even redemptive love (as if truly powerful or genuine love is only possible just this side of such obsession, perhaps even sometimes indistinguishable from it; or that the idea of romantic love *without* possessiveness, jealousy, idealization, and even some moral blindness, is all as great a fantasy as Benigno's. This is another similarity to Ophüls's *Letter*.) These are, in sum, the many different factors behind what I would suggest is our *hesitation* to characterize Benigno as finally belonging to the same category as the *Kill Bill* rapist.

Almodóvar is clearly aware that he is taking such risks and he marks the fact by opening the movie with Pina Bausch's avant garde dance, *Café Müller*. The part of that dance that we see is a mime of two women who are apparently blind, dashing about helplessly and eventually into walls, always threatening to stumble over the chairs in the café, aided by a man who frantically tries to move the chairs out of the way before the dancers stumble. But that particular Bausch dance as a whole is often much more violent, depicting romantic relationships as inherently aggressive, abusive, and catastrophic, and choreographing men and women frequently hurling each other into walls. Feminist critics have accused her of irresponsibility in presenting such dances without taking a strong position against such violence, and the dance critic Arlene Croce once wrote of Bausch's use of the "pornography of pain."

The silent language of dance also introduces the main abstract theme in the film: the relation between speech and silence; the main thematic terrain where the question of the film's credibility plays out. Speech and silence, both in themselves and as figures (often ironic ones) for agency and passivity or objecthood, must be considered within the many other such images associated with that theme—Alicia's comatose silence; the struggle against (silent) animals, brute "dumb" beasts (snakes and bulls); Lydia's silence with Marco about her resumption of her relationship with her former lover; the meaning of Marco's "expressive" tears (at both the beginning and end, and when he first meets Lydia and is reminded of his former girlfriend, Angela, a particularly angelic-looking actress); the silent movie, The Shrinking Lover, that images in some way the rape itself for Benigno; and then a final Bausch dance (Masurca Fogo), this time with a woman rising up from and floating above a line of reclining men, as if a soul set free from the body.

In such a context, it is clear that part of the point of the parallel plot with Marco and Lydia seems to be to emphasize the necessarily incomplete and even deceptive character of spoken conversation, how little gets communicated despite the conversations, especially in comparison with how much can be communicated in silent means. All of this emphasis tends to reduce our confidence that there is such a clear contrast between silence and speech, even "consensual" speech. In the central conversation between Lydia and Marco after the marriage of Marco's ex, Angela, at an extraordinary Andalusian baroque church in Cordoba, Marco is desperately trying to tell Lydia, finally, everything he had held back about Angela. But they are not really listening to each other. Lydia is herself trying to find a way to confess about her resumption with Niño, Marco realizes he has prevented something and covered something over by, ironically, for once trying to be so honest, by hogging the conversation and so forth. And there are several other examples that are meant to demystify the unquestioned value of speech itself as a vehicle of communication or sign of consent. This contrasting plot suggests that while it is mostly, it is not entirely ironic when Benigno says that his relation with Alicia has got a lot more going for it than most married relationships.

The bizarre silent movie is worth a bit of a digression here too. Originally Almodóvar had included more of the plot, which tells the story of the man's mother as a great villain. She had murdered the boy's father and kept him a virtual prisoner, until he was shrunk and liberated by the female scientist. This indicates even more clearly that Benigno views himself as liberated from his own mother by Alicia, even though she has caused him to diminish in stature, and that the scientist asleep figures in his imagination for Alicia in her coma, and that when he enters her vagina in a kind of reverse birth, he means to be there permanently, to die and merge somehow with the scientist.

Almodóvar, as he frequently does, cannot resist presenting some of this story as also an allegory of film and the relation of film to fantasy. There is a shot of the sleeping woman's face in close-up and of the little man in front of it that echoes almost exactly the scale of thirty-feet-high movie screens to normal persons, suggesting at once that Benigno's fantasy is an idealization and mythic exaggeration in a filmic sense, and that Almodóvar wants his own film to be viewed like that (expressionistic) silent film: somewhat surreal, more expressive than directly communicative, not a case study, as much at the very edge of moral intelligibility as the attempt to judge the acts of the shrunken lover.[12] We have to be careful here, because it is easy to mis-state the importance of this invocation of the inevitable role of fantasy in love, which all clearly has to do with the contrasting subplot. That is, Benigno is indulging a fantasy, projecting a movie in which the real Alicia can play no real part, contribute nothing. But—and this is the difficult point to state properly—in a more ordinary, less fantastical sense, so is Marco. Lydia is merely a character in Marco's re-playing the role of Angela, and in which Lydia's continuing love for Niño is not noticed, is ignored, even by her. She is in that sense, almost as "mute" as Alicia. None of this, of course, means that what Benigno does is the same as what Marco does, but this theme— Marco's repetition of Angela, Benigno's repetition of his relation to his mother, Lydia's repetition with Marco of her relation with Niño, Marco's repetition of the role of Benigno—is worth an independent discussion.

That Benigno thinks of his rape of Alicia in terms of the silent movie also helps us understand more of the pre-rape scene before Almodóvar cuts away. On Benigno's reading, Alfredo, the tiny lover, is entering his beloved's body forever, in some way merging with her. And we sense some unease as Benigno begins to form the intention to consummate his love of Alicia, something that clearly happens as he is massaging her thighs and recounting the movie. We don't sense any moral qualms on his part; just that he realizes that he is crossing an absolutely decisive line—after four years when it must have occurred to him often—and that there will be no going back. We don't exactly know why he thinks things have come to this, why just now they cannot go on as before, but he clearly realizes that now nothing will ever be the same. Given how meticulously he and the other nurses chart Alicia's periods, he might even know that she is likely to be ovulating and be intending to impregnate her, something that will clearly be discovered. If that is so then he sees himself in some fantasy as sacrificing himself for her, as if he knows, as he says later when he is in prison, "how it will come out," that she will have the child and re-awaken (but his life will be destroyed).

To return to the choice of the Bausch dance: it is in the face of this particular silent drama that the action of the movie begins. Marco weeps at this spectacle of the futile attempts of men to save women from their blindness and apparently great sorrow; perhaps by this point in the dance, he is also weeping at the futility of any hint of a successful romantic duet. But his tears appear to be an aesthetic response, evoked by admiration of the beauty of the attempt, not prompted by a sadness at the tragedy of failure. This intrigues Benigno, who happens to be sitting next to him, and who looks on in wonder as the tears stream down Marco's face. And all of this is a preview of sorts, since the dance is clearly meant as a foreboding account both of the suspended state of the two women in the story, Alicia and Lydia, dreamy, blind, as if floating in a void; as well as of the futile but passionate attempt of the male dancer, Benigno, to steer them away from harm, to continue attending to them. That Marco finds all of this so moving is an immediate attraction for Benigno, who has spent the last four years of his life spending all day and many nights ministering to Alicia's every need and, of course, talking to her.

The next day, he eagerly tells the story of this encounter to Alicia, clearly as moved by the tears as by the performance. And the film is off and running, creating the viewer's odd but undeniably strong bond with Benigno, and so the hesitation I have been discussing.

I conclude two things from these brief remarks. First, while Benigno's world is a pathological and ultimately destructive fantasy, aspects of his care for Alicia highlight, in a "mythical" way we might say, dimensions of the status of subjectivity itself. The premise of his actions seems to be that such personhood (and often gender itself) is a normative status, actively conferred rather than found, and that no "scientific" fact settles who is and who is not worthy of such status, and no mere performance can succeed in establishing such a role. As such, it is a status that can be denied or conferred, within social practices and in contexts too complex to allow for easy rules for guidance. Benigno's act always seems mostly altruistic, dedicated to Alicia, but as we all know, the fantasy that a vegetating person is still a subject, that she merits such status, can also be a destructive and self-serving, self-indulgent fantasy, and of course there are times when we end up not so sure about Benigno in this respect. (It seems to me an open question whether one could characterize this film, for all of Almodóvar's anti-clericalism, as still profoundly "religious.") We normally expect that such conferrals must be mutually recognitive to be successful, but the film works both to undermine our natural confidence that the verbal and explicit signs of mutuality, consent, and reciprocity are altogether trustworthy, and at least to suggest that such conferrals and sustained commitments are often required without the availability of such signs and that these acts of faith are dangerously extreme; they can easily tip over into the kind of unintended but real brutality of Benigno's rape. Love itself is sometimes treated as a species of this type, a "commitment" to another not driven by reflection or reason, something that can have a grip on one even if not reciprocated, never certain or securely established even when the commitment is mutual and "spoken." This is why the coma image also functions myth-ically: it raises the similar question of keeping faith with a beloved who has "gone away" in some way, has "become someone else," but who might return, go right again. (References to theatre, movies, and performing run throughout most of Almodóvar's movies, and have a lot to say about this theme. Such theatrical exhibitions are not treated as egocentric displays, manipulative forms of emotional control or phoniness, just by being theatrical; but rather as provisional forms of a kind of social address, vaguely interrogative, as if the characters are asking for a response that will confirm the role they want very badly to play. As in "if you treat me as a woman, I will be one," and the clothes and feminized behavior are therewith more interrogative, more aspects of a striving, than declamations; are requests to be so treated, sometimes requests offered plaintively, with a kind of pathos. Sometimes of course the external display is a mere disguise, quite unreliable an interpretive guide, as with police badges in *Live Flesh* or nun's habits in *Dark Habits*.)

The question of how socially instituted roles, even personhood itself as an instance of such roles, could be said to function successfully (or not) introduces an unwieldy number of large issues. But, in the same uncomfortable way in which Almodóvar is trying to render credible the idea of both condemnation of and solidarity with Benigno, he is deliberately trying to confound a number of the distinctions on which many such roles are founded. The most confounding involve his treatment of the dense, mutually implicative relations between subservience to (obsessive dedication to) another, and such subservience as also a form of mastery or domination. This comes out especially in the gender issue, as those roles are traditionally understood: that is, "womanly" men who function very much as males ("male" nurses) and masculine women who are also very much beloveds, fought over by men ("female" bullfighters). Or, of course, men with breasts, as in *Bad Education*.

Secondly, I have been suggesting that Almodóvar's treatment does not undermine a moral judgment of Benigno, but qualifies its ultimacy. This is a difficult point to make. First, we tend to mean a great many things by "morality," but I mean the modern residue of Christian humanism (systematized by Kant), where moral injury to another amounts to treating another as a means or object, making oneself an exception, and where moral agency requires a could-have-done-otherwise power of initiating action "because one decided to," and so where guilt or remorse at having failed to so treat others is the most typical or appropriate reaction. We tend to think of such considerations as *so* decisively trumping all other sorts of evaluation of acts or persons that any raising of such considerations can sound like a claim for diminished responsibility or a plea for excuses.

But the question is not excusing or forgiving Benigno, certainly not by appealing to any diminished capacity on his part or just by calling him beautiful or aesthetically successful. But what does anyone uncomfortable with what I have called our "moral hesitation" about Benigno really want? That Benigno be punished *more*? That Alicia remain comatose? That Marco abandon his friend in disgust? Would that make our response more acceptable? The question has more to do with de-coupling a moral judgment from the reaction with which it is deeply linked—blame, itself a kind of sanction that in most contexts seems inevitable, but here seems finally beside the point.

The movie works, I think, by concentrating a good deal of our attention on Marco's point of view and his reasons for neither abandoning Benigno nor, it is crucial to add yet again, excusing him at all, but for expressing some sort of solidarity with, even partly merging with, Benigno; and those reasons do not rest simply on pity for Benigno's deluded fantasy world. He seems to have learned that there is something redeemable at the core of Benigno's fantasy, that his care for Alicia, and especially his desperate attempts to "talk to her," were acts of faith that he was not capable of, much to his detriment, and that the rape, horrible as it is, still cannot be fully understood except within this pattern of daily, intimate four-year care.

But perhaps the crucial point is much more simple: that Marco has become Benigno's friend, indeed his only ever friend.[13] And friendships, like erotic love, are not subject to some sort of moral filtering, cannot simply be trumped by moral judgments about the "worthiness" of friends or lovers. (What would the world be like if they were?) What we are to make of this complication is not easy to see. As Marco, in the last scene, senses a future relation with Alicia, he knows he must eventually tell her the whole story of Benigno, and is naïvely convinced that it will all be, as he says to Katerina, the ballet teacher, "simpler" than one imagines. Almodóvar admits his own perplexity about all of this when he has Katerina, his filmic alter ego in effect, respond "I am a ballet teacher, nothing is simple," as we hear yet again an echo of those Kleistian angels who can also be devils.[14]

Notes

1 Stanley Cavell, The World Viewed (Cambridge, MA: Harvard University Press, 1979), p. 213.
2 Perhaps the Smiths' song from the 1980s, "Girlfriend in a Coma," also deserves a mention. (I am indebted to Jessica Burstein for this reference.)
3 We only hear the story about the mother from Benigno in the office of Alicia's father, a psychiatrist. He certainly could be lying or exaggerating; by telling the doctor that he washed his mother "front and back," he could already be trying to create his "cover" for stalking Alicia: that he is harmless because gay or has somehow been rendered asexual.

4 See P.F. Strawson, "Freedom and Resentment," in his *Freedom and Resentment and other Essays* (London: Methuen, 1974), and Jonathan Bennett's clear exposition in *The Act Itself* (Oxford: Oxford University Press, 1995), pp. 46–61.

5 There are of course other fantastic elements in the film drama itself; not the least of which is the way Alicia looks—her muscle tone, weight, complexion and so on—after four years in a coma.

6 Cf. Almodóvar's remarks: "Benigno is insane, but he has a good heart," and: "he's a gentle psychopath." Of most obvious relevance for this discussion: "His moral sense is different to ours, he's an innocent who, in his parallel world, has yet to reach adulthood." *Almodóvar on Almodóvar*, ed. Frederic Strauss (New York: Faber and Faber, 2006), p. 213.

7 All this is according to Almodóvar's commentary on the DVD version of the film.

8 There is also an amazing shot, a kind of close-up of the bull after the goring, that says something like: "I know I am supposed to lose, but you shouldn't have tried to show me up like that."

9 Again according to Almodóvar's commentary on the DVD soundtrack.

10 In fact, the relationship of the two men is more like a love affair than a friendship, romantically charged, if not physical. It is by talking to Alicia that Benigno finds something he has clearly never had—a deep friendship, but with Marco.

11 The role of friendship is stressed in another, related way in Almodóvar's comments: "I treat the character of Benigno as I would treat a friend," and: "It's like when a friend has done something terrible and you decide to turn a blind eye, just so as to keep them as a friend." And finally: "Deep down I like Benigno's moral ambiguity. I think he's one of my best male characters; and Javier Camara, one of my best actors." *Almodóvar on Almodóvar*, p. 219.

12 The same scale is shown in *Bad Education*, as the two boys and their first sexual intimacy is shown from the back of the movie house, with the huge melodrama dwarfing the real characters.

13 This raises another issue worthy of an independent discussion: why Marco agrees, at Benigno's lawyer's request, to lie, not to tell Benigno that Alicia has awakened. I don't think we are meant to believe that keeping this news from Benigno provokes his suicide (it might have been much worse for Benigno to know that Alicia was alive and that he was locked up and could not be with her). But it does raise as a question why, from Marco's point of view, he does not "talk" to Benigno about this.

14 Cf. *Almodóvar on Almodóvar*, in which Almodóvar says about *Talk to Her*, quite rightly I think, "But he [Benigno] falls in love with Alicia and that changes him, literally. As it would a child unprepared to live an adult love. In *Talk to Her*, Benigno is a kind of angel" (p. 213).

Chapter 4

George M. Wilson

RAPPORT, RUPTURE, AND RAPE:
REFLECTIONS ON *TALK TO HER*

P EDRO ALMODÓVAR'S *TALK TO HER* is a moving and
troubling film, but I have not found it easy to say clearly just what
is so moving about its larger perspective, and it is almost equally difficult to explain, without falling into an oversimplifying moralism, what
leaves one troubled in the end. Of course, the most disturbing action of
the story is plain. One of the two chief male characters, the hospital nurse
Benigno, rapes a comatose young woman, Alicia, a woman who is under
his professional care. The rape is shocking enough, but the fact that the
victim is completely unconscious and helpless can seem to make the

violation even worse.[1] Benigno's action is as close to necrophilia as is possible, given that the raped woman is technically still alive. And yet the movie, for the most part,[2] treats Benigno, as a largely sympathetic character; indeed, he is probably the most sympathetic figure in the film. More specifically, he is presented in the movie as the chief exemplar of a kind of fundamental human virtue. It is a virtue that the movie apparently endorses and one that the other male protagonist, Marco, notably fails to exemplify until his life is transformed by Benigno's example. It is the virtue of "talking to" one's friend or lover.

But, first of all, what is the virtue that is supposed to be in question here? Almodóvar, in an interview with A.O. Scott, warned him: "It's a bit of a contradiction that a movie that talks about words, communication, human voices is a movie that's difficult to talk about without betraying it,"[3] and the difficulty Almodóvar invokes is real. The virtue of "talking to" someone seems to be the virtue of establishing or trying to establish some fundamental mode of communication between the person who does the talking and the person to whom the talking is addressed. And yet, it is hard to imagine what sort of genuine and valuable "communication" is supposed to be even potentially achievable, especially in the situations that Almodóvar portrays in the film. As we will discuss later, much of the verbal "talking" in Talk to Her is represented as acutely problematic, a source of distortion, misunderstanding, and outright manipulation. Benigno seems to be an exception here. One may well have the impression that Benigno's talking to Alicia is offered as a paradigm of a loving and uncorrupted attempt to convey something absolutely vital to his patient. Perhaps this is so, but after all, Alicia is completely without consciousness, and the prima facie absurdity of Benigno's constant talking to her lies in the fact that communication with her in any familiar sense is apparently out of the question. If the virtue of "talking to her" lies in the achievement or even in just the goal of conveying something to the woman he loves, then it is hard to grasp what it is that could be expressed or otherwise conveyed to her. Even if we assume that the something that Benigno aims to communicate is something that lies beyond his words or beyond the content of any words at all, it should be possible to specify the general character of the way he seeks to establish some significant connection with her. Or, we can put the question in a different fashion. At the conclusion of the movie, Marco has apparently learned something crucial from Benigno about reaching out to another, but really, what is it that we are to imagine that Marco has come to learn?[4]

Moreover, are we really warranted in accepting Benigno as the embodiment of some basic virtue of compassionate human interaction? Whatever the mitigating aspects of the overall context might conceivably be, the fact is that Benigno rapes Alicia, and his action remains perverse and psychopathic even when the rape turns out to have some surprisingly fortunate consequences. In particular, one can worry that the movie is itself guilty of a certain rhetorical sleight of hand in its presentation of the rape and its aftermath. It is arguable that the way that the story is depicted allows us to avoid confronting fully and seriously what Benigno has done to Alicia. A key aspect of the concern is the charge that we are encouraged, in effect, to downplay the moral seriousness of the sexual crime. First, we are not directly shown the rape or any part of it. Instead, the rape is implicitly indicated on screen by an odd collision of abstract shapes; by the collision of the red globules that drift around in a lava lamp sitting next to Alicia's hospital bed. On first viewing, the audience simply cannot know the emblematic significance of these weird non-figurative images, and, on any later viewing, they signify the sexual activity in an oblique and purely symbolic manner.

Second, although Alicia becomes pregnant as a consequence of the rape and her infant dies when he is born, we also see nothing of these distressing outcomes. As noted above, it emerges, late in the movie, that the rape has actually had some surprising and positive effects. The childbirth seems to be the catalytic event that causes Alicia to awaken miraculously from her four years of coma. Further, in the final scene of the movie, there is some suggestion of the possibility for her of a new relationship with Marco, a relationship that, if it does develop, is likely to be redemptive for both of their heretofore disrupted lives. Nevertheless, in viewing the movie, we are effectively screened from the concrete reality of the rape, and we are offered the antecedently improbable idea that its upshot has been largely affirmative, at least for its victim. Are we really warranted in accepting this development as a sort of fortunate miracle, or should we reject it as an implausible and problematic narrative conceit? Really, how can this story, presented in this way, provide a reasonable basis for the supposition that Benigno embodies some sort of basic human virtue—a virtue whose importance Marco eventually grasps with life transforming consequences for him and possibly for Alicia?

Naturally, the answer to this question is bound to be particularly elusive if the virtue purportedly in question cannot be helpfully specified.

Of course, the rape is only one brief but critical episode in the long-standing relationship between Benigno and Alicia, and to begin to answer the two questions raised above I want to outline some major aspects of the way that their relationship is portrayed. Specifically, I want to stress the way in which, in the first half of the film, a strong contrast is drawn between Benigno's relationship with Alicia and Marco's relationship with Lydia. Benigno is the advocate, both in practice and prescription, of "talking to her"—of talking to one's friend or partner. And naturally, in his circumstances, his practice seems to be strange and irrational. Alicia is totally unconscious, and she has been in that state for four years. There appears to be no real possibility that she might comprehend or evince any other significant reaction to the continuing flow of Benigno's speech. In fact, Benigno believes or claims to believe that Alicia comprehends everything that he and others say to her, but clearly, this notion is absurd. At various moments, the absurdity is played for comic effect. At other moments, it has considerable poignancy, and the poignancy arises from the glimmer of a possibility that somehow he does make contact with her at some distant but still critical level.

Overall, it seems to me that Benigno's talking to Alicia is presented as an irrational but loving attempt to establish some kind of profound rapport with the loved one, despite the fact that neither he nor anyone else has any real conception of what that rapport might amount to. Benigno has a blind faith, against all evidence, that by caring for Alicia— by devotedly tending to her and talking with her—he can actually "convey" something to her. And, he supposes that by trying to somehow keep in touch with her, there is the hope that he can rouse her from her coma. He is unreflectively convinced that somehow she is touched in a vital way by his words and actions toward her.

"Talking to her," understood in the appropriate expanded sense, is a prime instance of and a metonymy for the activity of taking care of another person with unquestioning love, without any conditions and without expectations of reward or immediate response. In general, Benigno speaks to Alicia while he is constantly tending to her physical needs, her comfort, and her appearance, and all of these tasks are carried out meticulously, with incredible delicacy and expertise. Even if Benigno's verbal discourse to his patient often strikes one as ridiculous, one cannot doubt the value to Alicia of his skilful, devoted nursing. Whatever effect his words may or may not have on her, these ministrations help to keep her alive and in as much of a state of physical well-being as her lack of sentience permits. Even Alicia's psychiatrist father, who is otherwise skeptical of Benigno, appreciates the extra-ordinary benefits of the physical care that Benigno administers to his daughter. Moreover, even if Benigno's supposition that he is communicating with Alicia is nothing more than a pathetic illusion, his words express for him and for us the way in which this elaborate nursing routine is for him an activity of continuing love and dedication to someone whom he experiences as vividly present to him all the while.

Since *Talk to Her* strikes me as rather carefully structured around the unqualified importance of this sort of unswerving attachment and tacit intimacy, I believe that this topic needs to be situated within a broader setting that the film also elaborates—the possibilities and difficulties of *non-verbal* communication between two individuals. This possibility is central to Benigno's relationship to Alicia. Even if one dismisses the notion that Benigno communicates to Alicia with his words, it is harder to be sure that his purely physical ministrations to her do not establish some mutually sensed connection between them. Beyond this, the general question of non-verbal communication (of various sorts) is recurrently invoked throughout the film. It obviously figures in the opening and closing dance scenes and in the silent acting in the silent movie, and I will return to some of these scenes later. Moreover, there are a host of instances in which the success or failure of shared under-standing between characters turns upon whether meaningful visual or tactile contact has been established and upon whether or not the contact is mutually acknowledged. In fact, Marco initially attracts Benigno's sympathetic interest when Benigno notices the tears on Marco's cheek that have been elicited by the performance of the Pina Bausch ballet, *Café Müller*. And, at several later junctures in the movie, the sight of someone's tears is felt, sometimes rightly and sometimes mistakenly, to reveal something important about the depth of feeling manifested by the character that cries.

What is more, issues of non-verbal "communication" are not restricted simply to instances of possible communication between humans.[5] Thus, emotional connection figures in the evocation of the phobic power of snakes, and, more forcefully, in Lydia's dangerous interactions with the bulls. In the first bullfight, Lydia's proud, fierce stare and confident agility seem to convey her sense of mastery to the defeated bull. But the second bullfight is quite another matter in this respect. After Lydia has been struck down, there is an amazing shot in which the bull looks back in her direction as if to express his glowering contempt for her radical underestimation of his strength and danger. Before this disastrous bullfight, Lydia's sister attempts a superstitious mode of communication to another world when she constructs a shrine to saints in whom she is already losing faith. *Talk to Her* shows a variety of ways in which a person can come to be, or take him or herself to be, in significant touch with another creature even though no speaking has or could have taken place between them. Speech is presented as just one strand in a complex network of conventional and natural patterns of communication, and it is a mode of conventional communication whose unreliable nature is emphasized and elaborated.

Katerina, Alicia's ballet teacher, is an intriguing figure in this regard. She has a small but suggestive role in the story as a character whose gifts of intuitive, non-linguistic communication seem to far outstrip her capacities with concepts and with words.[6] She is, in the first place, a character who plainly cares a great deal for Alicia, and the depth of her distress and concern for Alicia is particularly established in the scene when she hears the news of Alicia's accident. She is literally shaken by the news. And, second, she is the only other character who accepts without self-consciousness or constraint Benigno's assumption that the unconscious Alicia should be talked to. When Benigno arranges the first of his "sunning parties" on the balcony of Alicia's hospital room, Katerina is a guest, and she speaks as naturally and comfortably to Alicia as she does to Benigno. Like Benigno, she treats Alicia without hesitation as if she were, more or less, a full participant in the conversation. However, it is striking that Katerina, in the context of this odd gathering, also comes across as a comic figure—sane, but addled and affected. Just as so much of Benigno's chatter has ranged from the banal to the goofy, most of Katerina's remarks are also unintentionally preposterous. Her description of the ballet, *Trenches*—the ballet of World War I that she is then planning to create—sounds pretentiously bizarre at best and, overall, Katerina tends to prattle on in an artsy, flighty, and sometimes word-challenged manner. Even in this scene, her considerable kindness is apparent, but it is doubtful that we are expected to take her very seriously here.

And yet, when Alicia, released from her coma, returns to the ballet studio, Katerina exhibits, as Benigno had, a loving concern for the recuperation of Alicia's body and spirit, and she is plainly prepared to take on some of the rigorous instruction and care that such a mending will require. So it may be that Katerina is not so good at verbal communication, but she, like Benigno, has some deeper feeling for the possibility of expressing oneself and communicating by other means and strategies. Katerina is Alicia's companion at the Pina Bausch ballet at the end of the movie. After Marco and Alicia have seen one another in the lounge, Katerina comes up to him anxious to know what they might have said to one another. Marco reassures her on that score, informs her that Benigno has died, and then, as she takes in the changed situation, says: "You and I should talk, and it will be simpler than you think." But Katerina seems somewhat skeptical about what the proposed talk might achieve. Her reply to him—the last words of the film—has considerable resonance. She states: "Nothing is simple. I'm a ballet mistress, and nothing is simple." And what she implicitly tells him with these words is certainly true: whatever hope that there may be for a restorative relationship between Marco and Alicia, there is no way that the realization of such a possibility will be simple.

Therefore, concerning the matter of "talking to" one's friend or lover, Benigno and Katerina are at least partially aligned. In contrast, it is crucial that Benigno and Marco, throughout most of the movie, are effectively opposites in relation to this theme. Marco simply cannot speak to the injured Lydia. As she lies in total oblivion, Marco waits in despair by her hospital bed. It is clear that he is emotionally shattered by her horrible injury, and he misses her intensely. Nevertheless, despite Benigno's repeated advice, he remains with Lydia in brooding silence and inaction. He waits, and he hopes for her recovery, but he doesn't try to talk to her. In fact, he can't even bring himself to establish any sort of physical contact with her. Of course, on first viewing, his unwillingness to speak to her is likely to seem altogether reasonable. Benigno is the one who seems to be an endearing and tender fool. Nevertheless, in the larger context of the story, Marco's silence in the hospital marks the limits and the inhibitions in his love for Lydia. In fact, one can wonder why Marco pays such long and faithful attendance on Lydia at the hospital, when there is nothing whatsoever that he thinks he can do for her. No doubt he has various motives for his continuing vigil, but there is the pretty clear suggestion that, because he presumes (wrongly) that he is Lydia's accepted lover, it is both his right and duty to remain there in bleak attendance to her. And he intends to claim that right and do his duty. However, El niño de Valencia, her previous boyfriend, will shortly explode that presumption for him.

It is essential to the unfolding of their story together that, even before the fatal bullfight, Marco has already failed, in a crucial way, to talk with Lydia. Just after they have attended the wedding of Marco's old girlfriend, Angela, we are shown an extended part of a conversation between them. Both at the beginning of the conversation and toward its end, Lydia says to Marco, "We should talk." The second time that Lydia tells him that they need to talk, Marco replies that, after all, they *have* been talking— they have been talking for the last hour or so. But, Lydia responds that *he* is the one who has been doing the talking. *She* hasn't been given a chance to say what she has on her mind, and she re-affirms that the two of them "should talk." It emerges only later in the film that she has decided to return to her previous lover, Niño. Her relationship with Marco has collapsed, and that is what she needs to tell him. But that vital information is suppressed. Marco is satisfied with himself—too satisfied with himself—because he means to be making both a confession and an important announcement to Lydia. For the first time, he talks frankly about the real depth of his old feeling for Angela, but he also announces that he has finally got past his debilitating obsession with her. This would be important news for Lydia if her feelings for Marco had not altered. But her feelings *have* changed, and now it is too late for him to learn that fact from her directly. Shortly after this conversation, she is struck down by the bull, and the calamity terminates all future interchange between them. There is a real breakdown on Marco's part in the course of this discussion. He is pleased with what he has to tell her, and he expects, reasonably enough, that Lydia will be pleased as well, but he is too self-absorbed to let her tell him what he needs to know. In the final moment of the shot in which the exchange between them is concluded, we see that Lydia turns and looks away from Marco. Their connection is visibly fractured by her simple action.

If Marco is centrally contrasted in this fashion with Benigno, a similar but less emphasized contrast is drawn between Marco, on the one hand, and Lydia's bullfighter boyfriend Niño, on the other. In the first part of the movie, Niño is presented as a pretty oily and arrogant character.

There is at least some suggestion that he may have exploited Lydia, professionally and emotionally, in their relationship. During an early scene in a bar, after the first of the bullfights in the movie, Lydia objects to a friend of Niño's that Niño has delegated the friend to speak to her concerning the apparent breakdown of their relationship and its consequences. Niño, it appears, is unable or unwilling to speak for himself in such a negatively charged personal situation, and, as Lydia points out, Niño has wanted the friend to speak for him. At this moment, the relationship between Lydia and Niño is shown to be in ruins. It is for these reasons, therefore, that it comes as a considerable surprise when it emerges that Lydia has decided a month before Angela's marriage to return to Niño. This means that she has kept this decision from Marco for a long time during the course of their relatively brief relationship. When Marco arrives at Lydia's hospital room and hears from Niño about the unexpected prior reconciliation between them, he stumbles upon his erstwhile rival sitting next to her bed and talking to her. Niño is holding her unresponsive hand and is avidly explaining to her his current circumstances and future plans. I think it is of great importance, in the scheme of the movie, that it turns out that Niño, whatever his other limitations, is capable of the kind of intense, unreflective endeavor to communicate with Lydia that Marco, despite Benigno's urgings, simply cannot undertake.

The first time I saw *Talk to Her*, I thought that Niño was lying. I thought that he was illicitly speaking for a person (Lydia) who has now been rendered incapable of speaking for herself. As noted above, he had, earlier in the movie, sent his friend to speak for him, and the issue of illegitimately "speaking for" someone else is a recurrent issue in the film. However, I now believe that I was simply wrong about this. If Niño is not telling the truth, then we just don't know what it was that Lydia wanted so badly to tell Marco before the bullfight. Moreover, the act of talking lovingly to someone incapable of hearing the words bears too much weight within the framework of values in the story to be easily discounted or dismissed.

There is a scene that pretty explicitly sets out how much may be at stake in the difference between Benigno's faith and Marco's contrasting despair. At the hospital, Marco has gone to see Lydia's doctor, Vega, to learn what the chances are that she will eventually recover. Dr Vega's answer is framed very carefully. He informs Marco, on the one hand, that there is no scientific basis for hoping for a recovery. The evidence overwhelmingly supports the conclusion that almost no one in such a condition will recover. On the other hand, he emphasizes that he does not mean to preclude the possibility of Marco's hoping that Lydia will awake. He points out that there has been at least one "miraculous" case of recovery from a coma similar to Lydia's, so recovery is not strictly impossible. Marco says, "So there is hope after all," but Vega responds, "No, I repeat, scientifically speaking, no! But, if you choose to hope then go ahead and do so." So there is always the alternative of hoping against all hope that a miracle will happen again. However, it is implicit in Vega's message that any such hope will have to be based on a combination of love and blind faith, since medical experience will not substantiate it. Now, Marco is a reasonable person, and he accepts the pessimistic, reasonable conclusion. Benigno has taken the alternative path with Alicia. Actually, it isn't that he has chosen to hope. He simply accepts that Alicia will recover and is unhesitatingly convinced that he is in intimate contact with her even as she lies unconscious in her bed. Marco is rational and resigned; Benigno takes the possibility of the miraculous on faith. In fact, earlier in the film he states flatly and as a matter of practical advice to another of Alicia's nurses, "I believe in miracles and so should you."

In the latter part of the movie, Marco discovers that Benigno's way was the right way, or, at least, he discovers that it represents the proper expression of one's genuine and committed love. Because of the deepening friendship between them and because of his own crucial failure of trust in the course of their friendship, Marco comes to see Benigno as the model of what trust and affection for another call for in a relationship with them. The crucial failure that I have in mind is this: it is, once again, a failure to "talk to" one's friend, honestly and without reserve. After Benigno has been arrested for raping Alicia and put in jail, Marco has a conversation with the new lawyer he has hired to represent the prisoner. The lawyer tells him what has happened to Alicia in giving birth to her child. The baby has died, but Alicia has astonishingly returned to consciousness. However, the lawyer warns Marco that Benigno should not be told this information. He is quite reasonably concerned about what Benigno might do if he were to know that Alicia has recovered. Marco is dubious about the subterfuge, but he agrees to suppress this news and asks the lawyer to speak to Benigno for him concerning the developments in Alicia's condition. It is understood between them that the lawyer will, in effect, lie for him. And, of course, Marco's failure to talk to his friend about the matter plays a critical role in bringing about the disastrous consequences for Benigno that ensue.[7]

Benigno can't bear the thought that he is unlikely to have any further contact with Alicia. If he knew that she was conscious, he could think that there was a possibility of some sort of communication between them, even if he were to remain in prison indefinitely. But, assuming falsely that she remains in her coma, he thinks that his imprisonment precludes anything like the connection that, in his view, has existed between the two of them. As a result, Benigno commits suicide by taking an overdose of sleeping pills. In a phone message to Marco, he tells him that he is planning to "escape," but Marco learns from the suicide letter that what Benigno has had in mind is an escape from life. He plans to escape into the dark void of coma, hoping to share that condition with Alicia before he passes from coma on to death. After Benigno's suicide, Marco reads the letter that Benigno has left for him and learns from it these consequences of his failure to tell his friend the truth. Reading the letter, Marco, the man who has cried so easily in the earlier part of the movie, breaks down in tears again. His earlier bouts of crying undoubtedly express real emotion, but the emotions in those settings often seem to be the effect of either an aesthetic response or of a distanced effect of some lingering, unhappy memory. On the occasion of Benigno's death, however, he cries profoundly, and his desolation is unmitigated.

In the penultimate scene of the movie, Marco stands at Benigno's graveside, and he talks to him. He talks feelingly and unreservedly to his dead friend—a person who is now even more surely beyond the reach of his words than Alicia and Lydia (in the hospital) ever were. Scenes in which someone speaks to a loved one at their grave are not uncommon in the movies. For instance, there is a famous and beautiful scene in John Ford's *She Wore a Yellow Ribbon* in which the John Wayne character, Colonel Nathan Brittles, tells his dead wife about what has lately been going on in his life. In Ford's *My Darling Clementine*, Wyatt Earp (Henry Fonda) goes to his murdered brother's grave and talks to him.[8] However, in *Talk to Her*, Marco's speech to the dead Benigno is, I take it, emblematic of the climactic transformation in him. As I have stressed, he has pretty consistently resisted Benigno's urging to talk either to Lydia or Alicia. It is something that, in its stark irrationality, he has not, with one tentative but notable exception, been able to bring himself to perform. The exception is this: after he has learned from Niño that he had reconciled with Lydia, Marco wanders down the hospital hallway, enters Alicia's room, collapses into a chair next to her bedside, and says, "Hello Alicia! I am alone again."[9] In fact, the remark is significantly ambiguous: to whom exactly are his words directed? In one way, Marco seems simply to be speaking to himself, and yet the first part of his statement ("Hello Alicia!") indicates that he is also, perhaps involuntarily, addressing his words to the comatose Alicia. In fact, I think his utterance is aimed in both directions. Out of old habit, he verbally formulates the painful upshot of his recent discovery to himself, and at the same time something in Alicia's presence draws him out and leads him to announce to her also that he is now on his own once more. This, it seems to me, is his hesitant and almost involuntary first step toward following Benigno's fundamental precept.[10] At any rate, by the time of the scene at Benigno's grave, all of Marco's old resistance to Benigno's advice has dissolved. He has learned the lesson of loving communication that Benigno has consistently both advocated and exemplified.

In the final scene of the film, Marco briefly meets Alicia at the theater. They have gone to see a Pina Bausch dance production. (In the movie's first scene, Marco and Benigno sat next to each other at a different Pina Bausch production.) It is seriously unclear what future relationship, if any, might be feasible for Marco and Alicia, but the tone of the scene is optimistic. Alicia looks at him almost as if she has some dim glimmer of recognition from the past, and she asks, "Are you alright?" He answers, "Yes. [pause] I don't know. [pause] I'm much better now," to which Alicia smilingly responds, "What?" Marco's reply to her has been incoherent, but it is quietly reassuring at the same time. Certainly, in my opinion, Marco has broken out of his earlier emotional constriction. He has come to be a person who is genuinely capable of caring for someone deeply—of loving Alicia with some of the same unconditional affection that Benigno has manifested toward her throughout. When Marco and Benigno meet together the last time at the prison, we are given indications of the direction and extent of the evolution in Marco's character. For one thing, the strong ties of real friendship are finally acknowledged on both sides in a direct and poignant manner. Their spoken acknowledgment of love for one another is completed by a joint gesture: Marco carefully places the palm of his hand on the hand that Benigno has pressed against the pane of glass that separates them in the interview cubicle. It is a significant gesture of fondness and solidarity despite the fact that, naturally, the glass between them prevents them from actually touching. The next time they are together Benigno is dead, and Marco visits his grave to talk to him again.

In the previous scene in which Marco visited the prison, the way that they are coming closer together in deepening friendship is symbolized as a kind of visual merging of the one onto the other. As the camera pans back and forth across the divisions of the cubicle, the reflection of first one man and then the other is superimposed upon the figure of the other. It is as if Marco can now see Benigno embodied in his own physical being and Benigno can see Marco in the same way, and it is the striking effect of the panning across the reflecting glass division that it makes it possible for the audience to see at least roughly what they are seeing in the other. More specifically, this visual effect yields the odd impression that Marco is sometimes speaking some of Benigno's words and that Benigno is speaking some of Marco's. In any case, it is in these two scenes in the prison that Marco moves decisively toward a genuine comprehension of his friend and the significance of their friendship. For instance, Marco can tell Benigno without constraint that it is fine with him if others think that he is Benigno's "boyfriend." After the emblematic moment of the merging of the two friends, Marco actually begins to adopt various aspects of Benigno's life before prison. He moves into Benigno's apartment, which Benigno had partially redesigned from catalogues to realize his rather dull, conventional ideal of a desirable domestic environment. Like Benigno before him, Marco begins to gaze out of the apartment window that looks out on Katerina's ballet studio across the street. And, to his surprise and ours, Marco sights Alicia (now miraculously recovered), who has come back to the studio to visit her former teacher.[11]

Moreover, it is clear that he is not only struck by seeing her again, but recognizes some growing feeling for her—a fascination and attachment that intensifies before they ever meet one another face-to-face. Their first face-to-face encounter takes place in the final scene of the movie, and, as described earlier, it occurs when they meet in the theater lobby at a Pina Bausch ballet. The fortuitous meeting is cordial, but brief and very tentative. It is as if both people sense that some implicit understanding already exists between them—a shared interest that it would be premature at just that moment to acknowledge or advance. In the final shot of the scene (and of the film), Marco is sitting in the last seat of one row, and Alicia is seated directly behind him two rows back. The last seat in the intervening row is empty, and the empty seat both registers Benigno's literal absence from the occasion and his symbolic presence in their lives at this juncture. Benigno and Marco had also first come into contact with each other at another Pina Bausch ballet about five years before, and Benigno, intrigued by Marco's tears, had recounted the notable incident to his unconscious patient at the hospital. Thus, the narrative-closing encounter between Marco and Alicia at the ballet is a variant repetition of the earlier encounter of the two men. The potential merging of Marco's life with Benigno's is defined at this juncture by the suggestion that Benigno's death may mediate the coming together of these two prospective lovers in an uncanny permutation of their previous relationships with Benigno and each other.

As I indicated above, the deepening of solidarity between Marco and Benigno in the prison scenes is crucial to Marco's larger emotional evolution at the film's conclusion, but that solidarity is also a triumph over the setting in which they meet. The prison is consistently represented as a place in which plain speech is liable to be monitored, grotesquely distorted, or otherwise inhibited. Indeed, it is an institution where any form of human communication is made difficult if not impossible. Given the basic value for Benigno of "talking to" another person, his punishment is arguably fitting, but it is also harsh. But, if the prison is the symbolic locus of inhibited exchanges, Talk to Her presents communication as an enterprise that is always under threat. Thus, for example, the movie shows us that there are many ways of talking with another person—most of them problematic and some even destructive.

The chief instance here, of course, is Marco's self-absorbed conversation with Lydia after Angela's marriage ceremony. Very early in the movie, however, there is a paradigmatic example of manipulative non-communication. Lydia has gone on a TV talk show, and the talk show hostess urges Lydia to talk about her relationship with Niño and its recent breakup, but this is something that Lydia absolutely refuses to do. In the terms of the movie, the hostess isn't really talking to Lydia at all; she talks at her, and talks in an exploitative and uncomprehending way. Indeed, when Marco first meets Lydia, he also wants to talk with her to get a story for his magazine. Similarly, Marco won't tell Benigno's concierge the whole story of the charges against Benigno and his resulting predicament, because she is too eager to tell her version of things to the "trashy" mass media. It is apparent that she is fond of Benigno, but she is also hugely disappointed that the TV stations and tabloids have not already arrived on her doorstep, asking for her version of the story. And, of course, it is a fatal turning point when Marco's negotiations with Benigno's first lawyer lead him to accept the proposal that he let the lawyer speak for him about what has happened to Alicia, thereby allowing the lawyer to lie to Benigno "for his own good."

And there are other ways in which even heartfelt, honest talk comes to be exploited. At one point after the rape, Benigno confesses to Marco that he wants to marry Alicia. And why not? After all, he affirms, they get along better than most other married couples do. Marco is the voice of reason here, and he is outraged at this ridiculous proposal. He warns Benigno that it is dangerous for him to go around talking in this way. Marco has more reason for his worry than even he knows at the time. It turns out that another nurse at the hospital overhears Benigno's declaration, and he subsequently tells what he has overheard at the hospital staff investigation into Alicia's condition. He informs the chief investigator that Benigno has expressed this fantasy of marriage to her, and he thereby seals Benigno's fate.

In the DVD commentary, Almodóvar asserts that Marco is the spokesman for the audience here and at other places in the film. However, I think that there are delicate issues concerning our intellectual and emotional alignments with each of the two male characters during the course of the story. In this scene, for instance, Marco gives effective voice to the natural reactions of the audience. He expresses the rational response to Benigno's wild proposal. "People talk to plants also," Marco says, "but they don't marry them." (Even Prince Charles, whose proclivities for chatting up plants are well known, has turned out to be no exception to the rule.) Nevertheless, I'm not sure that the natural reactions of the audience to Benigno's wishes are wholly endorsed by the film. Benigno is crushed by Marco's sharp rebuke, and he complains that he thought that at least Marco, his friend, would understand him on this score. I suspect that we *are* to discern a failure of comprehension in Marco's reaction.

It is not, of course, that Marco is wrong to reject the idea of Benigno's embarking on a marriage with a vegetative Alicia. Surely that idea is indecent and absurd. Nevertheless, Marco is failing to pick up the vital undertone of desperation in Benigno's declarations. He should recognize that something critical has happened to lead Benigno to feel that his continuing love for Alicia now needs to be consolidated in terms of marriage. He is deaf to this new tone from Benigno, and he reacts too harshly. If I am right about this, then audience members who too readily accept Marco as their spokesman in this scene may have also allowed their rational outlook on the topic to blunt their sensitivity to something that the movie is revealing to them in this moment. More broadly, we are right and rational when we judge that Benigno's rape of Alicia is morally repulsive. We are right and rational when we judge that Benigno's conception of his relationship with Alicia is an absurd delusion. But we have missed something crucial in the movie if these perfectly correct judgments preclude us from feeling some kind of sympathy and under-standing of—some kind of emotional connection with—the humanity of this deluded rapist. It is characteristic of much of Almodóvar's work that he asks us not to conflate our immediate reactions of creepiness and revulsion with the force of sound moral evaluations. And he asks us not to permit our moral evaluations, whatever their soundness, to preclude empathetic responses that might undermine or at least qualify the totalizing intensity of our "creepiness" reactions.

After all, it is not surprising that Benigno should have a radically defective conception of what marriage might entail. We know that the only important continuing relationship with a woman he has had occurred during the long period in which he nursed and attended to his mother. And, there is no question but that this fact about his youth has stunted his sexual and emotional development severely. We'll return to this point in a moment. However, the movie also makes it evident, although not with the same emphasis, that Marco's past romantic life has been problematic as well. He has spent years obsessed with the beautiful Angela. This obsession will not seem so very odd until we notice, at her wedding, just how very young she is. In fact, underscoring the point, Lydia comments specifically on this fact. What is more, if we remember that Marco states that the relationship with Angela has been effectively over for ten years, we have some reason to be taken aback. During the period that they were together, Angela must have been a teenager—probably a very young teenager at that. We learn from Marco in addition that the couple did so much traveling together mostly to keep her off drugs and away from the other temptations of city life. When Marco finally gives up on the relationship, he resolves the situation by returning her to her parents. Now, Benigno may be emotionally crippled, but what kind of serious emotional connection can Marco have had with an unstable, drug-addled adolescent? Perhaps, since he is a rational person, he can speak for conventional ideas of an appropriate marriage, but he is surely less than an ideal spokesman for the essentials of mature sexual love.

Benigno's conception of what a satisfactory marriage might involve is probably as banal as his taste in bedroom furnishings, but his experience of married life within his own family is more unusual. It has been truncated and grotesque. Apparently, his father disappeared from the scene early in his youth, and Benigno spent his adolescence taking care of his mother. As he explains to Alicia's father, a psychiatrist, these responsibilities to his mother fell upon him not because she was ill, but because she was "a bit lazy" and, having once been very beautiful, "didn't want to let herself go." We are never shown the mother directly, but we hear her cold, domineering voice when she summons him impatiently from his vigil at their living room window. We do see her as a lovely young bride in a framed wedding photograph upon the apartment wall. The picture has been framed in such a way that the bride is fully included in the visible image, but the husband has been almost entirely cut out. A bare sliver of his face lurks along one border of the frame.

The likely effects of this weird, oppressive family situation on Benigno's sexual psyche understandably horrify Alicia's father, and the state of his wounded psyche is the implicit subject of the bizarre silent movie, parts of which we are shown shortly before the rape occurs. The movie is called The Shrinking Lover, and Benigno recounts its plot to Alicia while we witness a selection of key moments from it. Actually, it is not entirely clear what we are supposed to be seeing when we see the purported segments from Shrinking Lover. Has Benigno actually seen such a movie? Certainly, we know that he has seen a poster for a movie with that title, but even the most Expressionist cinema of the 1920s did not really produce anything so peculiar in the manner of this film. Or, are we seeing Benigno's private fantasy of a movie he has seen—a private screening, so to speak, of his dominant psychological preoccupations translated into the idiom of a 1920s silent melodrama? Fortunately, it doesn't matter much what we suppose about this question. Either way, we can be sure that The Shrinking Lover enacts the troubled psychodynamics that are at work within Benigno. He admits to Alicia, as he begins to relate the story, that this is a movie that has really disturbed him.

The hero of this film within a film, Alfredo, is, like Benigno, somewhat overweight, and his girlfriend, Amparo, is trying to invent a diet formula. Alfredo drinks the untested formula (to prove by aiding her experiments that he is not as selfish as she thinks), but the concoction misfires in an unexpected way. On the one hand, it has the effect of unleashing his sexual passion for Amparo, but, on the other, it has the less fortunate effect of progressively shrinking him to the size of a mouse. When it appears that his shrinking can't be reversed, Alfredo, in despair, leaves Amparo and returns to live with his evil mother—a woman who has previously driven her husband away from the family home. Alfredo lives for an indeterminate period of time under the cruel domination of his mother. During this period he seems to have received some kind of important but enigmatic note from his departed father, but we catch only a glimpse of this and don't know what has been communicated to the son. In any event, Amparo is not so easily deterred by Alfredo's dejected retreat from her, and she rescues him from the mother's house. She carries him away, ensconced inside her purse. Reunited, the lovers check into room fifteen of the Hotel Youkali. While Alfredo scampers around the bed, Amparo lies there cheerfully and talks to him. Eventually she falls asleep, and her sleeping body is suddenly and overwhelmingly available to the shrinking man. It is for him a giant, luscious sexual landscape which he is free to scale, to scramble over, and to explore. When he notices her mound of Venus, Alfredo climbs down to the vicinity of her vagina, and, after some agitated hesitation, he climbs inside. His entry into her vagina is depicted as a source of intense sexual excitement for her and of a risky but attractive thrill for him. One presumes that his tremulous act of sexual spelunking is both the occasion of erotic gratification and, at the same time, a felicitous return to the maternal womb. Thus, the conclusion of The Shrinking Lover contains, as a piece of comic fantasy, the literalized enacting of the classic Freudian scenario of male sex. The fantasy, as depicted here, is funny, but at the same time, Alfredo's exhilaration and confusion mark out the utter ambivalence and incoherence of Benigno's sexual imagination.

Benigno's narration of the highly charged silent film is the prelude to his rape of Alicia, which takes place immediately afterwards. Up to this point in the discussion, I have given greater emphasis to the gentler, more compassionate aspects of Benigno's personality, hoping to locate their importance within the overarching value scheme of Talk to Her. But, of course, the central fact that he has violated Alicia complicates and considerably clouds the scheme as I have set it out. A major part of the reason that the movie is so fascinating and troubling is precisely because Benigno is not at all simply a 'benign' figure. He is a rapist, and, although we see nothing of the rape itself, just before the rape takes place we are shown some expressions of his more frightening and dangerous impulses. In the course of telling Alicia about the movie, Benigno is giving her an elaborate massage. In one shot, he is meticulously massaging her lower torso, and just after he finishes his account of Shrinking Lover and tries to explain his reactions to the film, the massage is now directed at one of Alicia's inner thighs. This second shot of the massage especially offers us a more chilling view of Benigno as he looks slightly dazed, disturbed, and sexually aroused. And then, the movie abruptly cuts away from him to the oozing red forms that drift within the bedside lava lamp. This is an especially important moment in which his darker, more threatening side has been pretty overtly manifested in his countenance and behavior. These signs in Benigno's demeanor portend the impending rape, although this is a fact that we learn only as the film progresses.

Further, this is not an isolated moment. First, we have already learned unsettling facts about the beginning of his obsession with Alicia. It was formed initially in silence and in the absence of any personal contact with her, having its basis in attraction and fantasy. He had picked her out among the students at the dance school across from his apartment, and he had spied on her dance lessons for long hours afterwards. We know that he had slyly contrived to slip into her home and to steal a hairclip from her bedroom as a kind of talisman of his desire for her. Alicia bumps into him during this episode, and in this last experience of him before her accident, she is terrified by his incursion. So we have seen something of his iron determination to establish some private, even magical link to her despite the fact that this involves an unwanted violation of her personal privacy and its potential cost of alienating her completely.

After the rape occurs, we intermittently see something more of his cunning, his anger, and his pride, and, in the late part of the film, the steelier side of his character is displayed in his still grimmer determination not to be completely separated from her forever. As such, these traits may actually deepen and reinforce some sympathy for him, but, if so, whatever sympathy we feel is likely to be ambivalent. He never expresses remorse for the rape, and his unremittingly devoted obsession with Alicia can seem to be little more than a mode of self-absorption. That is, he is fixated on a figure that he has created largely in fantasy, basing the fantasy on the few fragments of information that he has gathered about Alicia's tastes and interests. In fact, the fixation and the frustrated fantasy seem only to intensify during the period he is in prison.

The larger vision of *Talk to Her* seems to be roughly this: a caring, intensely devoted man, acting out a welter of confused passions, rapes the comatose patient he adores. The act is vile, but, by a kind of miracle arising from the man's spiritual influence, it brings about redemptive results both for the woman and potentially for his male friend. The miraculous outcomes are the product of a terrible violation, but the positive miracles constitute a legacy, not of the action, but of the unreflective devotion of the man. It is as if the loving character of his spirit has inscribed itself across the subsequent history of his crime.

At the beginning of this chapter, I raised two general questions. The first, in effect, was this: how are we supposed, in the end, to understand Benigno's commitment to Alicia and its legacy? I have suggested that the core of that legacy lies in his embodiment of the virtue of 'talking to' another person in the right way and with the right sort of receptive consideration. But again, how might that virtue be more fully explained? To some extent, we probably should not expect that it *can* be adequately explained. In the end, there is an element of mystery about the kind of fundamental communion that Benigno tries to establish with Alicia. When Benigno first tells Marco that he (Marco) should talk to Lydia, Marco asks Benigno to explain what he has in mind. Benigno replies, "You have to pay attention to women, talk to them, be thoughtful occasionally, caress them. Remember that they exist, they're alive, and they matter to us." Perhaps these prescriptions are too close to conventional sentiment to be very helpful, but they plainly endorse a special sort of empathetic openness to signs from the other of what they need and want. And this receptiveness is to be conjoined with a willingness to respond with equal openness to those signs, providing thereby an acknowledgment of the living reality of the other person and the value of his or her life. Finally, this openness in perception and action is to be sustained even in the face of contrary evidence and despite the negative mandates of common sense. In any case, this is the best positive characterization that I can give.

The second question I raised was: to what extent are we warranted in accepting Benigno as the exemplar of such a virtue? He is a troubling and troubled character at best, a character who is capable of an atrocious act. Does the movie make it too easy to accept its culminating perspective by deflecting us, in the peculiar way that it tells its story, from the full impact of what Benigno has done and from some of the most painful consequences of his deed? Here again, I believe that each viewer will have to sort out his or her own feelings about Benigno and his curious history. Nevertheless, there are two points that I would urge in thinking through an answer to this second question.

First, if *Talk to Her* were offered to us as a realistic case study of the actions of a sexually ambivalent male nurse and his friend, then our warrant for seeing Benigno as a paragon of anything would be dubious. But naturally, it is not presented to us in this way. In the opening shot, a theatrical curtain rises on the stage for *Café Müller*, but it equally and emphatically rises from the surface of the movie image itself. As this odd shot suggests, the film is offered as a piece of theater, a theatrical piece in which the realistic, the melodramatic, and the comic are woven together. And, just as the opening dance number stages a parable of affliction and desperate attempts to provide some assistance and relief, the movie also offers us a kind of parable—a "moral fable," of, say, perversity and its unpredictable relations to human well-being. Now, it may well be that some will have difficulty accepting the movie even in these terms, but it is important at least to grasp the nature of the imaginative framework that the movie seeks to establish.

Second, Almodóvar has stated that, at least in his early films, he had an "amoral point of view," and I take him to mean that he was unconcerned in those films with moral evaluations of his characters and their deeds.[12] Certainly, many viewers have thought of him as an amoralist of some ilk. However, I cannot see that, in *Talk to Her* at least, he proposes some kind of amoral perspective on its action and on the rape in particular. It seems to me that one is entitled to judge that the central act of rape is unequivocally immoral and to permit that judgment to figure centrally in one's reaction to Benigno. Indeed, it seems to me that the movie does not ask us to imagine that the rape is either excused or mitigated by Benigno's emotionally stunted youth. A strong, negative moral judgment is a natural and correct reaction to this central incident in Benigno's life.

Nevertheless, the film also insists that the moral judgment should not obliterate other aspects of our sympathetic responses to the man. In particular, it does not give us reason to set aside or give less weight to the rare, empathetic virtues that Benigno has been shown so constantly to exemplify. It is true that it is not always easy to be sure to what extent Benigno is motivated by a superogatory devotion to Alicia, on the one hand, and by a rather repellent obsession with her on the other. This difficulty of discernment creates the largest continuing ambiguity in our possible reactions to Benigno and the film. Nevertheless, such epistemic uncertainty does not mean that we cannot distinguish between the two types of motivation or that we are doubtful about which we value and which we deplore. It is my impression that, for Almodóvar, Benigno is a kind of genuine saint;[13] but in Almodóvar's world, sainthood is fully compatible with bizarre fetishization and even crime. We may struggle to keep our conflicted responses to Benigno straight, but *Talk to Her* does not require that we conflate the moral and non-moral considerations upon which those responses have been based.[14]

Notes

1 The fact that Alicia is unconscious and completely helpless when Benigno rapes her does makes the rape especially disturbing in certain respects, but Connie Rosati has stressed to me that, because Alicia is in a coma, the rape actually lacks certain other characteristic features of rape that are themselves quite terrible as well. First, Benigno is obviously not forcing Alicia to do something against her will, and it is not his aim to humiliate her or to cause her to experience his subjugating power over her. Second, he is not circumventing her will as he would be if she had been conscious and, for instance, he had administered a drug that inhibited or destroyed her capacity to try to resist. These and related considerations may qualify our specific reactions to Benigno's rape, but they will not alter our judgment that the action is morally wrong.

2 The qualification "for the most part" is important here, and later in the discussion I will consider some of the amendments that need to be added. I believe that the audience's relation to Benigno is meant to be predominantly sympathetic, but it is also critical that one is bound to feel considerable ambivalence toward him as well. This ambivalence is one aspect of the movie that generates its complexity of emotional tone, a complexity that is hard to describe adequately. But I will explore this issue at some length later.

3 The interview was originally published in the *New York Times*, November 17, 2002. It was reprinted as "The Track of a Teardrop, a Filmmaker's Path" in

Pedro Almodóvar Interviews, ed. Paula Willoquet-Maricondi (Jackson: University of Mississippi Press, 2004), p. 163.

4 I owe to Connie Rosati my sense of the importance of this blunt formulation of the question.

5 Jerry Dworkin singled out the significance of this topic for me, and it deserves a more elaborate investigation than I can give it here.

6 Gideon Yaffe proposed to me this way of understanding the character.

7 Gideon Yaffe pointed out how often the failure of one character to tell another something that the former knows and the latter ought to know figures in the development of the plot.

8 At the beginning of Almodóvar's 1997 movie *Live Flesh* (*Carne tremula*) an infant is born on a bus, and at the end of the movie a child is born in a taxi, both vehicles driving through the streets of Madrid. The child born on the bus is one of the male protagonists, Victor, and the child born in the taxi is his son. In both cases, a character talks to the as yet unborn child, encouraging the infant to emerge. It is Victor who talks in this way to his own child, telling him that he is coming into a much better world than the world into which he (Victor) had been born. So, even here we have a striking example of affectionate but unreasonable "talking to" another being who cannot possibly comprehend the words.

9 Dick Moran emphasized to me the importance of this remark as an early and critical turning point in Marco's movement toward Benigno's point of view. It is worth noting that earlier in the film, when Lydia asks him if he is single, Marco says to her: "I am alone." It is an odd way of answering her simple question, and I take it that, in both instances, it is Marco's condition of emotional isolation that is being underscored.

10 When Marco first sees Alicia in her hospital room, she suddenly opens her eyes and seems to stare at him. Benigno explains that this is a purely automatic reaction that occurs intermittently in the comatose. Since Alicia is still in her coma, she is not responding to Marco and does not see him. Nevertheless, in light of their potential coming together at the film's conclusion, this moment can be read as symbolizing a special attunement between them that is supposed to exist at some level from the outset.

11 For a wonderful close analysis of this sequence, see John Gibbs, "Looking, Talking and Understanding: Subjectivity and Point of View in *Talk to Her*," in *Close-up 01*, ed. Douglas Pye and John Gibbs (London: Wallflower Press, 2006), pp. 54–68. This analysis occurs in a section of his longer essay in the *Close-up* volume, "Filmmaker's Choices." Gibbs starts out with a marvelously detailed and rich account of the sequence in question, but he proceeds to a fuller interpretation of the film as a whole. I found his discussion extremely insightful and provocative. Although there are many significant points of overlap between his viewing of *Talk to Her* and mine, there are also some striking differences. It would take a rather long essay to

work through the points of similarity and difference, but the Gibbs essay is strongly recommended to readers of the present volume.

12 For instance, in an interview with Victor Russo (in *Film Comment*, November/ December, 1988), Almodóvar says: "I like big melodramas, but I can't actually make a big melodrama because my point of view is amoral." However, he may only mean that he can't accept the kind of prevailing morality that, in his view, lies at the basis of "big melodrama." This interview is also reprinted in the collection cited in note 3. See p. 66 in this volume.

13 It is interesting to recall the odd exchange between Marco, Lydia's sister, and her husband about certain missionaries in Africa. The two men claim that these missionaries have taken to raping the local nuns because they are afraid that the native women might be HIV-infected. The rapes performed by the missionaries have an added dimension of atrocity because their actions obviously desecrate the most basic values that they hypocritically profess to represent. Benigno's rape of Alicia, by contrast, has a touch of personal pathos: it violates not only the woman, but also the fundamental, compassionate virtue that Benigno basically represents.

14 I have had a lot of help with this chapter. I received incisive comments from Robert Pippin, Michael Fried, and Louise Antony, when the paper was first read at the APA session in Chicago. Jerry Dworkin, Dick Moran and Gideon Yaffe read early versions of the paper and made a range of very helpful suggestions, only some of which I have been able to take up in the text. Moran also saved me from a couple of embarrassing errors. Connie Rosati also read an early version and sent me written comments that have had an extremely valuable impact on the final draft, an impact that extends well beyond the points acknowledged in earlier footnotes. Finally, the biggest influence on the paper came from Karen Wilson, with whom I have discussed the movie a gazillion times. In fact, I talk to her a lot.

Chapter 5

Cynthia Freeland

NOTHING IS SIMPLE

PEDRO ALMODÓVAR'S FILM *TALK TO HER* (*Hable con ella*) offers an extended rumination on the nature of persons and human relationships. Its narrative shows two vibrant women cut down by accidents of fate and reduced to mere bodies in vegetative states. Each woman had singularly inhabited or animated her body before the tragic event that led to her being comatose. The younger one was a promising ballet student, the older one a successful and daring bullfighter.

The problem of minds, or of whole people, who get reduced to mere bodies has some connection to the problem of objectification. It is commonly held by feminists that men tend to "objectify" women, though it is less agreed just what this means and whether or why it is bad.[1] In the most typical and I hope uncontroversial sense, to objectify someone means to treat her simply as an object and not a subject. Feminists complain that men regard women as mere bodies to be observed or used for sexual pleasure, rather than as persons in their own right. Thus Catharine MacKinnon writes: "To be sexually object-ified means having a social meaning imposed on your being that defines you to be sexually used, according to your desired uses, and then using you that way."[2]

This would appear to be an appropriate worry in a film where a crucial plot development is rape by a lead male character of his comatose and inert female patient. While we might be tempted to say that this is what is disturbing in *Talk to Her*, I don't think such an analysis is actually correct or helpful. It is interesting to ponder why not, because it will show us some things about the understanding of persons in relation to our own moral outlook. For one thing, the male nurse almost alone among the hospital staff and visitors regards the two comatose patients as actual persons and not mere bodies. He sees them still as the women they were and as having a larger potential as human beings. He remarks early on in the film: "You've got to believe in miracles." Even when he cares for his patient at the most basic, surely disgusting bodily level by washing her and cleaning away her bodily discharges, he still regards her as having a psychology, preferences, attitudes, emotions, moods, and so on.

Whether we are obligated to treat a comatose person as a subject or true person is itself controversial, as was demonstrated by the recent uproar in the US about withdrawing life support from the long-term comatose patient Terri Schiavo. The relevant sense of a moral requirement might stem not so much from our current belief that the comatose person is a person as from respect for the person that they *once were*. It is along these lines that Kant argues we owe respect to corpses due to the persons they have been. *Talk to Her* complicates our moral reaction to the rape because the ensuing pregnancy does appear to result in a miracle, awakening the victim so that she is able to return to her life and, importantly, to her dance classes.

That the rape is nevertheless clearly wrong, and that the seemingly sympathetic nurse Benigno emerges as a monster, affords a different understanding of what is really wrong with objectification. True, it is important for us to treat other humans as subjects rather than objects, but this film suggests that there is more to our duties than just this, since Benigno clearly does see his patient as a person. This is why he keeps talking to her and insists that his friend Marco do the same for his comatose girlfriend Lydia. The film's position is that we have to do more in order to truly "subjectify" a person: we must "get them right." That is, we have to work to see the *actual* subjects that they are, and not the ones we *imagine* them to be. To do so requires an almost endless effort at interpretation and re-interpretation.

This means that people are very much like works of art themselves (including, obviously, films). *Talk to Her* calls for its audience to grasp this basic message in an especially salient way by reviewing, re-watching, and re-interpreting scenes we saw earlier and found innocuous. Our mistake, if it was one, in liking and trusting Benigno is not something that can be corrected by the alternative slogan "listen to her." Instead, I will argue, it should be "interpret her." The film offers us some wrenching moments of moral darkness and pain as it poses its fundamental challenge to us as its viewers: to engage in this fundamentally human project of interpretation and re-interpretation.

The film presents the two women as both subjects and objects by highlighting their physical embodiment of self. Both women are performers in disciplines that involve careful choreography and strict adherence to physical disciplining of the body. When they are alive, fully inhabiting their bodies, they lend themselves an animation that they strikingly lack when they become comatose. We develop a relationship as viewers and audience members to these women—both to the characters depicted and the actresses who portray them, through a visual and kinesthetic awareness of their bodies. The scenes of their animated performances in dance or the bullring are linked to scenes of other artistic performances throughout the film. I begin with the important fact that the film both opens and closes with scenes of dance performances.

The dance sequences

To be more precise, *Talk to Her* actually begins by showing the image of a closed curtain. It slowly rises to reveal the stage of a theater where, as we later see, an audience is seated watching a dance performance. The final scene replicates this, again in a theater but without the parallel of any closing curtain—something that we must consider significant. These scenes are important both to the narrative and symbolically. They emphasize the theatricality of the film-watching experience, suggesting parallels between the on-screen audience members and ourselves, in particular between the chief character, Marco, and ourselves. Given that the curtain does not actually close at the end, the film suggests that the process of watching and understanding the artistic portrayal (of either dance or film) does not have any real closure. These key dance sequences emphasize the film's fundamental message about the challenge in the interpretation of the behavior of others—in particular, how to "get at" what is inside their bodies, their "real selves," if you wish.

Both the initial and last dance sequences show portions of works by the contemporary German choreographer Pina Bausch, leader of the Tanztheater Wuppertal. In the opening sequence we see part of Bausch's work *Café Müller*, in which she herself is performing along with another female dancer, Malou Airaudo. At the very start, just after the curtain rises, we in the film audience see a close-up of the anguished face of an older woman. As she begins to move, she seems to be sleepwalking or stumbling about in a nightmare. Both women on the stage move in this jerky, somnambulist fashion. They wear white slips and are constantly on the verge of stumbling into the disordered tables and chairs of a black café. A slender man tries frantically to keep them safe by removing obstacles from their path. Each woman falls against a wall and collapses, then gradually rises.

Though the gestures and setup of *Café Müller* include comedic elements, the mood is overall very somber. Certainly, no one in the depicted audience laughs. The emotion of sorrow is intensified by beautiful late Renaissance opera music, the soprano aria "O Let Me Weep, For Ever Weep" from Purcell's opera *The Fairy Queen*. This opening scene is important for several reasons. Symbolically, it foreshadows the film's suffering and sadness—in particular that of women, but also the desperate attempts of men to save them. Like the two female dancers, the film's female protagonists will both fall into comas after terrible accidents. And the film's male leads will struggle to love and care for these women.

Narratively, the scene depicts the accidental meeting of the film's two male protagonists, Marco (Darío Grandinetti) and Benigno (Javier Cámara), strangers who happen to be seated next to one another. Marco reacts to the dance's intense emotion by silently weeping, which is noticed by the sympathetic Benigno in glances stolen over at his neighbor's face. This sequence suggests that Marco is very emotional and that Benigno is observant and empathetic. This latter feeling is reinforced as the setting shifts abruptly from the scene of the performance to Benigno's narration of it the next morning as he cares for his patient Alicia (Leonor Watling) in hospital. He mentions the weeping man to Alicia and describes the performance. (Benigno also remembers Marco later on when they meet at the hospital.) He tells Alicia that the dance was the saddest thing you can imagine. It takes some time for the film to reveal that the person he is talking to is showing no response. We realize that she must be very ill or in a coma. As the sequence unfolds, Benigno and another nurse wash her body, then dress her in a nightgown that resembles the slips worn by the dancers in Bausch's piece.

One can see why Almodóvar would choose this performance as the stage-setting for his story. It foreshadows the story of the movie's characters. The two women in the film, as in the dance, in effect become sleepers as they are struck down by their respective accidents. The men try to take care of them—in effect, to remove obstacles facing them. Both men turn out to be repeat caretakers: Marco had protected his previous girlfriend Angela, trying to shelter her from drug use by taking her away on trips with him. And after he first meets Lydia González (Rosario Flores), the famous lady bullfighter, he wins her confidence by killing a snake in her kitchen. Benigno, obviously, nurses Alicia, his patient, just as he had previously cared for his mother for many years.

The film concludes with selections from a work of an altogether different sort, the *Masurca Fogo* (Fiery Mazurka) by Bausch (1998). This is a much more recent and complex dance suite of which we see only two portions, shown here as occurring just before and after an intermission. Unlike *Café Müller*, this more recent suite is romantic and lyrical.[3] It employs an eclectic mix of soft, often sad music, including a lament sung by kd lang, "My Baby's Gone," as well as some sexy and upbeat Portuguese folk tunes. The mood of the end of *Talk to Her* is both narratively and metaphorically far more optimistic and positive than at the film's beginning, despite the tragedies that have occurred in the course of the story.

In the selections we see from *Masurca Fogo*, romance seems more of a possibility, although it also involves the risk of pain and loss.[4] The first selection, shown before the intermission, is very languid. It shows a group of men who gracefully pass along the body of a woman in a red dress—a siren of sorts. She is almost limp, held over their heads as they pass her along. She holds a microphone as if about to speak or sing, but says nothing, instead offering up breathy notes. What we do hear is k.d. lang's sad lament as she sings, "I woke up this morning. . . . it slowly dawned on me my baby's gone."

Again, the sequence functions narratively because it depicts another important meeting among the central characters. Alicia is in the audience, sitting with her dance teacher, Katerina. Marco sits a few rows ahead of them. He is once again moved to tears; this time it is the sympathetic Alicia who notices that he is crying. Symbolically, the sequence could allude to the fact that now Alicia has awakened from her coma, because of a pregnancy, but one that involved the death or loss of her baby. Or it might refer to the loss of Marco's friend Benigno, who was also the "lover" who "woke up" Alicia but who is now gone, after committing suicide in jail. Indeed, Marco's emotions seem to spill over from the immediately preceding scene in which he visited Benigno's grave.

As the audience files into the lobby for intermission, Katerina offers Alicia an interpretation of what we have just seen: "Waves. Cruel waves, the male below, the female above." The mood of this portion of the Bausch piece is quiet, but I am not sure that Katerina is correct or is meant to be an accepted authority. We have heard her earlier describing plans to choreograph a major dance suite which will involve a cruel war between the sexes. So she may be bringing her own "issues" to the interpretation of Bausch. In describing her planned work earlier to Benigno and (the comatose) Alicia, Katerina says that it will depict a battle scene during World War I. The women will wear long white gowns like the Wilis in the classical ballet *Giselle*. She says that the ballerinas will represent the souls of the men. Her piece will show cosmic processes: from death emerges life; from the male, the female; and from the earth, the ethereal.

As I have mentioned, Alicia has noticed Marco's sadness and, as they sit nearby in the lobby, she leans over to ask if he is all right. Katerina sees them talking and shows concern for Alicia by whispering to Marco as the audience returns to the theater, to ask what they talked about. "Nothing," he replies. He also warns her that he is now living in Benigno's apartment and that she might see him in the neighborhood of her dance academy. Katerina seems cautious and tells him, "One day we should talk, you and I." Marco responds by saying "Yes, and it will be simpler than you think." But Katerina quickly corrects him: "I'm a ballet mistress—nothing is simple." This, the last remark of the film, is hard to interpret. I take it to mean that talking and trying to engage genuinely with another person is, like ballet, an art that takes skill and long hours of training, practice, and hard work. Still, the possibility of a new and more successful romantic relationship is hinted at by the title over the screen just before the film's final section, "Alicia and Marco." Significantly, it is shown in very small letters, as though hinting that this is just a mere possibility.

With Katerina's words serving both to finish the film's dialogue and as a preface to future developments, the movie concludes with another sequence from Bausch's work. The mood lightens and becomes sexy as a line of couples emerges from the left, dancing together across the stage. The women wear folksy dresses and have their backs to us. The music is up-tempo, happy and flirtatious. We see Marco and Alicia watching with enjoyment, and then they even exchange a smile. The couples on stage gradually separate and depart until only two people are left, a boy and girl who seem to be talking and flirting. The setting is idyllic; a full-screen photographic backdrop depicts lush trees and a waterfall. The end credits begin to roll. Perhaps this final couple is emerging into a newly forged Garden of Eden, the garden after the fall. We have to remember, Marco did kill the snake.

Women's bodies in *Talk to Her*: active and inert, alive and comatose

Talk to Her is a male-orientated film, focusing on men's problems in understanding, loving, and being involved with women. Perhaps his sexual orientation as a well-known "out" gay man even heightens Almodóvar's interest in showing men's puzzlement about women and their "mysterious brains." The movie depicts an unusual, tender, and complex developing friendship between two men who are otherwise loners with problems sustaining emotional connections to others. Let me turn now to the ways in which the film depicts its two female leads.

On the one hand, we are often led into voyeuristic scenes regarding their bodies as pleasurable objects of visual interest. Alicia's body, in particular (that is, the body of the young actress Leonor Watling), is often displayed for the viewer's enjoyment, as the camera caresses her supple limbs, smooth flesh, soft thighs, shining hair, lovely cheeks, plump lips, and delectable breasts. In one scene she is even posed on her side with a graceful languid arm laid along her hip, odalisque-like. Once when Marco has stopped to stare at her through a half-open door, Benigno chides him, "Admit it, you were looking at her breasts, weren't you?" Our voyeuristic point of view can seem problematic if we realize that it is echoed in various behaviors of Benigno. He is shown in flashbacks in numerous scenes watching Alicia at the dance studio across the street from his mother's apartment. He arranges a visit to her psychiatrist father so that he can sneak into the family's living quarters and spy on her when she emerges from the shower. Her situation in the coma is all the more poignant because when she first meets Benigno when he returns her wallet, she tells him passionately: "I couldn't live without dancing."

Though there is no similar visual lingering on the naked body of the other lead woman, the bullfighter Lydia Gonzáles (Flores), there is certainly a magic associated with how the camera treats the remarkable face and figure of this woman (in real life a famous Spanish singer). She conveys the impression she would be a good bullfighter by her posture and manner in the bull ring. We see Lydia twice in the process of being dressed by her male assistant as she is elaborately wrapped and prepared for the bull fight. Her slim feet, long legs, tiny waist, and small torso are beautifully displayed in the matador's braided and bejeweled outfit, as is her remarkable long nose, heightened in profile by the bullfighter's traditional hat and by the hairstyle she wears, long black hair tightly wrapped in back. Lydia is quite differently depicted at times when she wears flowing sleeveless gowns, with her long lean arms making elegant gestures. Hers is another sort of beauty from Alicia's. Rather than being modern and young, Lydia has the narrow profile, large nose, strong brows, and dark staring eyes of an ancient Iberian queen—like the sculptures that inspired Picasso to create several of the women in his revolutionary painting Les Demoiselles d'Avignon.

There are two bullfighting scenes featuring Lydia in action. The first is closer to the film's opening, and, as with the dance scene, Marco is in the audience watching. This scene is both lyrical and painful to watch, much like the Bausch opening sequence. (I think it uses the same music.) We see Lydia fighting in tight relation to an exhausted and bloodied bull;

they both move in slow motion. Lydia is obviously well aware of the bull's presence and danger, but gracefully eludes him as he moves back and forth across the screen and across her body. The bull is sweating and in obvious pain. Lydia stares at him in direct confrontation, then glances toward her audience in triumph.

The second bullfight has an altogether different outcome, as this time Lydia is the one wounded, not the bull. Again, she is perfectly dressed and coiffed. She prepares herself to receive the bull by assuming a kneeling position directly in front of the entry chute. I have read that this is a standard position in classical bullfight repertoire, albeit one that is considered unusually daring. The camera cuts from her pose to overhead shots of the bull, snorting, impatient, and huge inside his box, being goaded to increase his rage. When he comes charging out at her, it is all over in a flash as he gores her and tosses her now-limp body like a rag doll.

It is important that Almodóvar shows women actresses who "inhabit" their bodies so fully during their scenes of living animation before becoming comatose, in order to dramatize the terrible difference in their states before and after. This heightens our emotions of fear and pity for them. The story, as I have hinted by use of these key words, takes on dimensions of ancient Greek tragedy. But just who is the hero whose downfall the story narrates? There are two ostensible heroes, Marco and Benigno; one survives, the other does not. They both suffer tragic losses during the film, but only one seems guilty of the error or *hamartia* that leads to his downfall: the unconscionable act of Benigno's raping his patient, Alicia. Marco also comes to feel guilty in the sense that he eventually realizes he has not listened to Lydia, who wanted to "really" talk to him just before the fight that would disable her. She was about to tell him she was returning to her previous lover, the bullfighter Niño, but was unable to because Marco filled up the time instead by telling his own story. Marco also never quite "heard" the reality of Benigno's feelings for his patient Alicia.

The tragedy that befalls the two women is significant, of course, but in the movie it serves the end of helping to unfold the tragedy of the two men. This tale is not so much about the women as about the men. This might seem to reinforce the point with which I began, that it is a story that objectifies women in the sense of using them as objects for a further, deeper purpose. The women become blank and unconscious, unanimated bodies in order that the story of the men's friendship and tragic loss can itself unfold. This might lead to a negative assessment of Almodóvar and a criticism of him for yet again making women into objects to serve the male gaze and male moral development.

But that would be an unfair complaint. The movie is about male friendship and also about men trying to know and understand women. It is about achieving authenticity in human relationships. It shows how difficult this is but holds out hope at the end of something better—a more fruitful, open and honest interchange that will come about after the tragedies of the movie. Recall the meeting and conversation at the end between Marco and Alicia, when their two names are linked by a screen title, just as other pairs of names have been linked earlier in the film, hinting at a future romance. We hope that Marco's loss of both Lydia and his friend Benigno has educated him, and that he realizes the importance of Katerina's reminder that "nothing is simple."

As a woman with considerable experience of the world and of life, Katerina knows that things just aren't easy, either in life in general or in the world of her dance students in particular. Her remark may also mean that in the world of art, nothing is simple. A new artistic rendering of the relationship between Alicia and Marco would itself need to be complex and shaded. It's not going to be all that easy for the two of them. Alicia may well feel resentful, for example, upon learning that Marco was close to the man who spied on her and then raped her while she was comatose.

The animated body

What would subjectification of a body amount to, if it is the reversal of the sorts of behaviors that feminists criticize? On a subtle and interesting characterization developed by Martha Nussbaum, objectification involves a variety of behaviors, such as regarding another's body as an instrument, denying their autonomy, and more.[5] Working from Nussbaum's list, "subjectification" would require the following acts and attitudes that are opposed to features she cites as objectifying: not regarding another's body as an instrument; accepting their autonomy; recognizing them as active and not inert; treating them as unique not replaceable; accepting their boundaries; not treating them as something to be owned; and recognizing their subjectivity.

A dancer and bullfighter are obviously active, not inert, as are the actresses who are performing in the roles of Alicia and Lydia. But are they truly autonomous, unique, and characterized by intact bodies? We could argue that the dancer's body must always be subjected to the dance and its choreography. Bullfighting, too, is about danger and risk: the body can suddenly, shockingly become inert if it is horrifyingly pierced by the bull—as occurs in the fearful scene where Lydia is hurt. Similarly, actresses like Watling and Flores must give their bodies over to the camera for examination and use. But the crucial thing is that these are all meaningful performances in which a person is communicating through their body. It is natural for people to use their bodies to reveal or express their subjectivity, their autonomy. What people do in their art is the same as what they can do, ideally, in sexual activities. That is, they lend themselves to their bodies and to bodily experiences, whether of practiced movement, pleasure, or pain and suffering—in a way they cannot do once they have become comatose. This is what makes Benigno's rape so monstrous and helps explain why Marco confesses that he now finds Lydia's body "disgusting"—it is a mere shell of a human, something like a corpse. Without her animating it, her body is not "her" anymore. Despite what he imagines, she cannot participate in making love to him.

The idea that subjectification involves the animation of a body and communication through the body's movements is clearly exemplified in the arts of ballet and bullfighting. These arts reinforce the idea that understanding another person as a subject involves more than just magical mind-to-mind telepathy between two Cartesian thinking substances. One might imagine that we can relate to a person just by "talking to her," that this is a way to find out what's inside the "mysterious brains" of women. But the film shows that this is far from true. Its title is a deception, quoting the advice given in the film by the man who turns out to be a rapist. Marco had *talked to* Lydia, but failed to listen or to understand her needs and emotions. Benigno *talked to* Alicia, but had no concept of her needs and desires.

What might have helped each man was to interpret how the women acted—how they moved, how their bodies communicated. Lydia faced danger with her body, but she was always more daring than she should have been in order to prove things—first to her father, himself a failed matador, and later to her matador boyfriend Niño. A man comments to Niño during the first bullfight scene that Lydia is taking too many risks,

and adds, "She'd let the bull tear her apart just so you could see it."
Alicia's interactions with Benigno reveal her fear and suspicion, first when
he walks beside her on the street seeking to return her dropped wallet,
and even more so later on when he stalks her at home. Her body and
facial expressions should have shown him what he never could recognize:
that she found him creepy and frightening. As viewers, we can be lulled
into forgetting this because of the obvious loving care he demonstrates
in tending to each part of her—cutting her hair, massaging her face,
giving her pedicures, washing her breasts and genitals. All of this loving
attention seems to contrast favorably with Marco's revulsion from
Lydia's comatose body. But in fact, the latter reaction is more natural,
since it is distressing to see the body of someone one has loved become
inert or uninhabited. This is something many of us might know from
dealing with incapacitated elderly family members, if not comatose
loved ones.

Skepticism about the value of "talking to her" is also foreshadowed
by a scene near the start of the film in which we are introduced to Lydia.
She makes an appearance on a talk show hosted by an obnoxious TV
personality. The interviewer tries to make Lydia discuss her breakup with
Niño, but Lydia refuses, even when the woman presses her by saying:
"It's good to talk about things, and talking about problems is a way to
overcoming them." Lydia obviously disagrees and actually tears off her
microphone and storms off the stage, leaving her hostess comically
grasping out to restrain her from leaving. Lydia's behavior "talks" for her.

The challenge of interpretation

Talk to Her is a self-consciously theatrical film. We are frequently shown
scenes depicting performances and emphasizing audiences' emotional
responses. These include the dance performances, television show, and
bullfighting sequences that I have already discussed. Another extended
scene shows the comical silent film Amante Menguante, and there is a
beautiful wedding where a congregation watches the young couple get
married. In the silent film, the shrunken man explores the nude sleeping
body of his scientist girlfriend as if in a weird dance or athletic event,
climbing its mountains and exploring its depths. Similarly, the wedding
sequence depicts the familiar "dance" as participants parade down the
aisle in ritual costume.

In another scene showing a party at a country estate, the singer Caetano Veloso mesmerizes his audience with the sad but beautiful "Cucurrucucú Paloma." Strangely, the scene begins abruptly with a somewhat abstract shot of a swimmer diving into water. This shot is out of context and serves, I feel, to conjure up emotions of sensuous pleasure and exploration of bodily rhythms. It is tied to the mesmerizing tones of the singer's lament for a lover who has left home, leaving behind only the dove that symbolizes her soul.

In many other scenes the lead characters become watchers: both Marco and Benigno spy on Alicia at the dance academy across the street, and Marco watches Benigno and Alicia from a balcony in a room across from theirs at the hospital. In many of these scenes the audience is moved emotionally. Usually this involves Marco, but at the wedding it is Lydia who weeps. These accumulated visions of theatrical performance support my claim that the director is emphasizing ways in which human beings present themselves to others and occupy certain roles requiring constant attention, response, and interpretation.

Marco has to be taken as the film's key figure, both hero and audience surrogate. We experience his rollercoaster of emotions as he becomes fascinated by Lydia, is distanced from her inert body, finds friendship with Benigno, and is attracted to Alicia's poignant beauty. Marco is also the person who stands to benefit, if anyone can or will, from the tragedies of the film. Has he learned anything from his utter mis-understandings of Lydia and failure to talk to her, or from his sympathetic friendship with the man some see as monstrous, Benigno? Like Marco, we too probably evolve from finding Benigno a sympathetic and kind caretaker to a sinister predator. Marco is a travel writer, a person whose specialty is to be a tourist in other places and then describe the experi-ence so that others can share it vicariously, as they plan their own trips. Tourists merely visit places, they don't settle down there. And indeed Marco, as an Argentinian, is a visitor to Spain. Yet by the end of the film Marco has taken over Benigno's apartment and may be settling into a new life.

I have discussed the way in which the camera treats the bodies of the two actresses who portray Alicia and Lydia, but we should also consider the male actors and their physical embodiments. Much of the weight of the film is borne by the extraordinary acting of the two leading men. Grandinetti is completely unlike the somewhat boyish and slightly tubby

Cámara. Marco is lean and rugged—the nurses at the hospital talk about how sexy he is and speculate that he must be well hung. He has a handsome if unusual face, with a receding hairline, intense dark eyes, and a thin, ascetic look. Just as Lydia resembles one of the Iberian classic beauties who appear reborn in Picasso's art, so does Marco remind one of a saint or scholar from the fifteenth-century Netherlandish artist, Rogier van der Weyden. Almodóvar often closes in on his striking face with perspective and lighting. There is an especially powerful extended shot of Marco in Benigno's apartment after he realizes that Alicia has emerged from her coma. Grandinetti's face is shown at an unusual three-quarter profile, its angles highlighted against the deep reds of the background.

An important issue for Marco is whether he can shift from being an isolated weeping member of an audience to becoming more genuinely involved with anyone—either a close male friend or a female lover. I would like to think that the screen title "Marco y Alicia" near the movie's end hints at a hopeful answer to this question. After all, for the first time, Marco is actually sharing a response to the performance with someone else—both when Alicia expresses concern for him at the intermission and later, when they exchange smiles after the sexy line dance. Perhaps Marco has been moved by the horrific tragedy of what Benigno did and suffered to a greater maturity. Marco had fallen into utter emotional isolation when he went to Jordan to continue his travel writing, leaving Lydia behind in the hospital for Niño to visit and watch die. But that ends when he hears of Benigno's being jailed. Frantic with concern, Marco returns and rushes to the prison. In two wrenching scenes when he is able to visit Benigno they cannot make physical contact. One of the saddest moments in the film is when Benigno tells Marco, "I haven't had many hugs in my life." Marco may have been hugged, but he has not had any more direct emotional contact with someone than Benigno has. But perhaps this is the one positive outcome of the entire long tragedy of the film: Marco may have learned that in life, as in art, nothing is simple.[6]

Notes

1 See Catharine MacKinnon, "Feminism, Marxism, Method, and the State: Toward Feminist Jurisprudence," *Signs* 8 (1983): 635–58.

2 Catharine MacKinnon, "Human Sexuality: A Feminist Political Approach," in *Theories of Sexuality*, ed. James H. Geer and William T. O'Donohue (New York: Plenum Press, 1987), p. 78.

3 In fact, this piece by Bausch has been seen by critics as a sign that the choreographer is mellowing. A *New York Times* critic writes:

> "Gone are the days of the all-too-ugly battle of the sexes," announced one critic. Another wrote that the artistic director of the Pina Bausch Tanztheater Wuppertal "has become gentle," displaying a "new and almost old-fashioned tenderness." Kissing couples abound, as do scenic projections of erotically bursting petals and shivering stamens.
>
> Ann Daly, *New York Times*, October 31, 1999. Available at http://www.anndaly.com/articles/bauschmellower. html, accessed October 1, 2006.

4 See this excerpt from a review:

> *Masurca Fogo*, a piece first developed for the 1998 Lisbon World Exposition in celebration of Pina Bausch's company's twenty-fifth anniversary, opened at the Brooklyn Academy of Music in October of 2001. It can easily be said that *Masurca Fogo* is perhaps one of the lightest of the choreographer's productions, a break from her angst-ridden vision of human relationships and the human predicament.
>
> Babak Ebrahimian, "*Masurca Fogo* (review)," *Theatre Journal* 54:4 (December 2002): 653–4.

5 Martha Nussbaum, "Objectification," *Philosophy and Public Affairs* 24 (Fall 1995): 249–91.

6 I am grateful to Vanessa Voss, Tom Wartenberg, Josh White, George Wilson, and Marcelo Zigaran for their comments on earlier versions of this paper.

Chapter 6

C.D.C. Reeve

A *CELEMÍN* OF SHIT: COMEDY AND DECEPTION IN ALMODÓVAR'S *TALK TO HER*

FROM THE WINDOW OF HIS APARTMENT, Benigno Martín looks down into the ballet academy across the street. His gaze is fixed on Alicia Roncero, a beautiful young dancer doing barre exercises under the direction of her teacher, Katerina Bilova. Soon, an impatient voice calls him away: "Benigno, you've been at the window for half an hour." It is his mother. To the right of the window, we see an oddly cropped photograph of her as a young bride. At the end of the film, when it is out of its frame, in Benigno's prison cell, the oddness is explained: it is half of a wedding portrait from which the bridegroom's image has been crudely torn.[1] Next to it on the prison wall is a photograph of Alicia.

The screen fades to black. Again, Benigno is at the window. But this time there is a difference. His mother has died, and so he is free, as he wasn't before, to go out when he wants to. He sees Alicia kiss two friends goodbye at the academy door. As she walks off, she opens her shoulder bag and her wallet falls out. Benigno runs down, picks it up, and follows her. For a few moments he walks along silently beside her. She speeds up. He keeps pace. When she eventually confronts him, he explains about the wallet. It is the beginning of a long scene that is as carefully choreographed as the two Pina Bausch ballets—Café Müller and Masurca Fogo—that serve as the film's bookends. In no other scene do a man and a woman seem to be in such near perfect communication, listening attentively to one another as they talk about their loves and lives, charting effortlessly the obstacles a busy city street poses. Watch it in slow motion; watch Alicia's face as she looks into Benigno's; watch the flow of their coordinated movements. It could be the beginning of a love story. Which is just what—in its own strange Almodóvarian way—it turns out to be.

She loves dancing, Alicia says, and going to the cinematheque to see silent movies, and traveling. Until his mother died two months earlier, Benigno responds, he has been too busy taking care of her to do much else. Her mother is dead, too, she replies, "but a long time ago." Then, with a quick "we're here," she steps into the fast-moving traffic. We share Benigno's anxiety as we watch her turn to wave from amidst the cars and trucks, and then make her way safely across. The honking horns remind us of other horns and the dangers that they pose to beautiful women. When Alicia has entered the building, he follows and notes the apartment she rang: "Dr. Roncero. Psychiatrist. 7th. Left." Their brief conversation will become the template of his new life, in which ballet and cinematheque will figure. But by the time it does, travel will be out of the question, because Alicia will be in a persistent vegetative state in Woodlands clinic (El Bosque) and he will be her nurse, as he was his mother's before.

Again, Benigno is at the window watching for Alicia. When he repeatedly fails to spot her, he calls her father's receptionist to make an appointment. "I just wanted to see Alicia again," he tells his friend Marco Zuloaga, to whom he is narrating the event, "but as I was there, and her father was a psychiatrist, I decided to tell him that I missed my mother." His subsequent session with Roncero reveals just how strange his life has been. For fifteen years, we learn, he was his mother's nurse and beautician: "I cut her hair, dyed it, did her nails, and I scrubbed her down well, front and back. My mother wasn't disabled or mad. She was just a bit lazy, you know? My mother was beautiful and I didn't want her to let herself go." Benigno's fast, light-hearted delivery makes his account seem comic—everyone laughs at "she was just a bit lazy." But what he is describing isn't funny: a depressed, once-beautiful mother, who has lost her will to keep up her appearance; a young son, who becomes that lost will, washing her "front and back," and devoting his entire life to her. Roncero's next question is ours, too: "What did your father say to all that?" But his father wasn't there to say anything. He abandoned his wife when his son was five and formed a new family in Sweden.[2] Benigno never hears from him. The torn photograph is now partly explained, and also, no doubt, some of the mother's depression.

When Roncero asks Benigno what problem has led him to see a psychiatrist, his answer is: "Loneliness (*la soledad*), I suppose." When Alicia took his mother's place, he was "not alone (*solo*)" anymore. When he is no longer allowed to see her ("they're doing some tests, but they won't tell me anything"), loneliness becomes a problem again:

BENIGNO: I wanted to talk to you about that before you leave.
MARCO: About what?
BENIGNO: Loneliness. I want to get married.
MARCO: Married? Who to?
BENIGNO: To Alicia, of course.

Marco is outraged: "The woman is in a coma!" "We get along better than most married couples," Benigno replies. It's a funny line. But the humor is ours, not his. What he knows of love is what he learned at home. A depressed mother, a comatose wife . . . each needs a love that breathes a will into her, much as a character in a film needs an actor in order to come alive. "I've hugged very few people in my life," Benigno tells Marco. He means that he hasn't been hugged much—that love for him has been a one-way street. "I really identified with those people," he says, "who've got nothing and invent everything."

Finally, with a sense of at last cutting to the chase, Roncero turns to sex. When he discovers that Benigno hasn't had a lover, male or female, he suggests they meet again:

BENIGNO: Why? Am I not well?
RONCERO: No, it isn't that, but your adolescence was what we might call special.
BENIGNO: It wasn't that special.
RONCERO: It was. Very special.
BENIGNO: Well, whatever you say.
RONCERO: And we should analyze it more deeply.
BENIGNO: Yes, we'll analyze it.

It is another instance of one-sided comedy. Benigno takes the word "special" in one sense; Roncero intends it in another. Benigno is so funny, indeed, so apparently self-assured and competent, that we tend to take him at his own estimation of himself as someone with whom nothing is wrong—even in contexts like this one, where we have good reason not to.

When Benigno leaves Roncero's office, the receptionist isn't at her desk. Down the hallway, through a semi-opaque glass wall, he sees Alicia taking a shower. Passing shelves filled with antique toy cars, trucks, and motorbikes, he picks one up and looks at it. We are reminded of the ominous traffic from the earlier scene: the threat is now inside. The door to Alicia's bedroom is ajar. Benigno goes through it. We see clothes on the bed, the right-hand bedside table, with its yellow lava lamp in the shape of a spaceship and its replica of the Eiffel Tower, the dance photographs above her bed. On the left-hand table, the camera pauses. There is a matching red lava lamp, a photograph of Alicia's parents as a young couple, and one of Katerina, who loves Alicia "like a daughter." Next to them is a Spanish translation of Davis Grubb's The Night of the Hunter. The photograph on the cover is of Robert Mitchum playing Harry Powell in Charles Laughton's film adaptation. Powell's left hand, with the word "HATE" tattooed on the fingers, is just visible. In the dramatic sermon he regularly stages, the right hand, tattooed with "LOVE," wrestles it down. But in his life, hate always triumphs. Dressed in the clothes of a preacher, Powell is in fact a psychopath—a hater and killer of women. The orderly clothes disguise the sexual disorder within. That Alicia should be reading Grubb's book will turn out to be a complex irony. That we see she is reading it is something else: a warning. Like the lamps and photographs, it too will be in her room in Woodlands.

Pocketing her hairclip as he steps into the hall, Benigno runs into Alicia herself half-naked, her hair still wet from the shower. Startled to see him, she clutches her bathrobe around her to cover her breasts. "Don't freak out," he tells her, "I just wanted to see you. But I'm harmless." She nods her head quickly in assent. She believes him so completely that she doesn't report the incident. We believe him, too, despite the warning that we have been given.

With Alicia watching, still a bit shaken by the sudden encounter, Benigno hurries off. As he leaves the apartment, a door opens and the receptionist steps back to her desk. She picks up the ringing phone: "Dr Roncero's office. Oh, hi, Lola. I've just taken an elephant-sized dump (una mierda como un celemín)." Alicia, a look of confirming disgust on her face—she knows the receptionist, obviously—returns to her bedroom. The scene works with English subtitles. In Spanish, according to Almodóvar himself, it fails. "Now comes a verbal joke, which is not funny," he says in his commentary (included on the Sony DVD), "because no one knows what a celemín is. A celemín was a unit to measure wheat that has no relation to the metric system. A celemín of shit means a huge amount of shit, like might come from a cow." Inside Dr Roncero's apparently elegant receptionist, in any case, is something grossly animal, something that exceeds the rational order represented by her own carefully contrived exterior, and—as we now know—by the metric system. The joke, in other words, amplifies the warning. Orderly appearances can be the deceptive whiting on something unsavory.

Roncero's beautiful designer apartment, his Eames chair and Eileen Gray table, his art collection, his immaculate clothing—are they whiting too? When Woodlands recommends Benigno as a nurse for Alicia, Roncero hesitates only briefly. "When he saw me," Benigno tells Marco, "he remembered that we'd met and he had a moment of doubt, but he ended up hiring Mathilde and me exclusively." Four years go by. Then an incident occurs. Benigno is massaging Alicia's inner thigh with his knuckles. *We* see that there is nothing improper about it. But when Roncero happens upon it, alarm bells go off. Referring back to their first conversation, he asks Benigno about his sexual orientation and whether he likes men or women. Knowing what is on his mind, Benigno lies to him: "To answer your question in some way I think I'm oriented more towards men." Satisfied that Benigno is no threat to his daughter, Roncero leaves him to finish his massage.

Benigno is soon being funny about the incident with his nurse friend, Rosa—"Did he ask the head nurse if she's a dyke? Did he ask you if you like bestiality or coprophagy?" But that shouldn't make us complacent or blind. Roncero knows Benigno's history. Yet he takes what he is told at face value, reporting it to others as gospel. "Are you insinuating Benigno's a faggot?" Rosa asks the head nurse. "I'm not," she replies. "It's *vox populi*, honey . . . Dr Vega confirmed it for me . . . Alicia's father told him." A good psychiatrist, especially one concerned about his own daughter, would surely have been less doctrinaire, more perceptive and circumspect. Roncero is the one character, indeed, that Almodóvar seems to parody. In a film where "the person who talks is the one who loves," it is noteworthy that he never talks to Alicia.[3]

The brief scene with Roncero's receptionist is tied thematically to another brief scene. Marco is in a hotel room in Córdoba, waiting for his lover Lydia González, who is a professional bullfighter. Soon she will be getting ready to meet the bull that will put her in an eventually fatal coma. With Marco are Lydia's manager, her sister, who is setting up a portable shrine, containing images of Jesus and of Lydia's dead father, and her sister's husband, Antonio:

SISTER: Did you read about the nuns? The ones who were raped by the missionaries in Africa. The priests themselves. It's horrible. If you can't trust a missionary, what's to become of us?

MARCO: They used to rape the local women.

SISTER: Really?

MARCO: Because of AIDS, they started raping the nuns.

SISTER: Oh, my God! And I used to have the missionaries on a pedestal.

MANAGER: I'm sure not all of them are rapists.

SISTER: I hope not.

ANTONIO: No, some are pedophiles.

SISTER: What's that?

ANTONIO: Everybody loves fucking.

SISTER: Shut up, Antonio. You're such a brute.

Again, the exchange is funny, but not the topic. Like Benigno, like Roncero and his receptionist, like Harry Powers, the priests are not what they seem. Their devout exteriors conceal something bestial and black—something their religious training is powerless to control. The sister's own acts of outward devotion, too, stand in sharp contrast to her irreverent words. You must have faith, the manager says, when Lydia is in Woodlands. "I keep lighting candles," the sister replies, "but I'm finding it hard to believe."

The photograph of Lydia's father, prominent in the shrine, is one Lydia also keeps on the hall table of her house: the camera lingers on it. He wanted to become a bullfighter, she tells Marco in their first conversation, but "he stayed a *banderillero*," encouraging her to succeed where he had failed: "'Not the girl' (*el niña*)," Lydia's sister says. "My mother and I were always telling him that. But she turned out just like him." Even the name he gave her (the *lidia* is the entire *corrida*, but in particular the part involving fancy play with the cape) testifies to his ambition: "it was like sealing your fate," Marco says. What he means is soon explained.

When we see Lydia in the bullring for the first time, a black-and-white photograph of a man lying in bed, swathed in bandages, momentarily fills the screen. It is Manolete (1917–47), one of the greatest bullfighters in Spanish history. Lydia's fighting style—characterized by an upright stance, fixed feet, holding the red cloth *muleta* backwards and low, allowing the bull's horns to come close to her torso—identifies her as his acolyte. Soon we will see Lydia herself lying bandaged in a hospital bed, dying from wounds that she received in the city of Manolete's birth. Marco, who is confessedly ignorant about bullfighting, can hardly have been aware of all that. But Lydia's father is a different story. Like the bull, he was blinded by the fancy play with the cape to the dark thing it conceals. One of Manolete's major innovations was to do away with the *lidia*.

When we think of fate, it is often as a magical power. Fate here isn't magical. The father wanted a son to fulfill his ambitions. A loving daughter takes the missing son's place. To make her way in a man's world, she must show herself more macho than any man. She models herself on Manolete and takes huge risks: "Two bulls, six, whatever they say." Her name becomes linked to him and his history. Thrown together with bullfighters, she falls in love with one, leaves him for Marco, and then returns to him. Nominally, he is the brother she never had: she is *el niña*, he *El niño de Valencia* ("The Valencia Kid," as we might say). It's as if her father's desire for a son, like his desire to be a bullfighter, has also become hers.

To enter the bullring, Lydia must put on men's clothes. Back in the hotel room, we see her being dressed in them. The camera lingers on the beads and brocade, the buttons and buttonhooks, the lovely pink stockings. It shows us Lydia's naked torso and its old scars. This time the animal within is "the soft animal of your body," as Mary Oliver calls it, which can suffer and die.[4] The costume is culture, custom. It hides the soft animal, giving it an air of invincibility. It turns killing a beast into an allegory of culture's consoling triumph. We see Lydia in the bullring making practice passes with the cape. We hear the trumpets sound. A man in the black costume of a *banderillero* takes his place behind a protective wooden barrier. It is the place of the father. But the real supporting father is dead. Lydia kneels in front of the gate, her ornate cape in a semi-circle in front of her. Her legs spread wide apart. She is adopting a position— *porta gayola*—that is seldom taken till late in the fight when the bull is tired, since it restricts movement so much. We see the bull in the chute. We see the *banderillas* being stuck in his neck and shoulders to madden him. We see Lydia take out one of the gold medals she wears around her neck ("she never took them off," Marco says). The image is of Christ on his way to be crucified, the cross on his shoulders, his head crowned with thorns. Once he has put on the clothes of flesh, even a god is subject to pain and death. We see the bull from above as it enters the bullring. A great black muscular lump, it almost fills the screen; not a *celemín* of shit this time, but what it represents.

In a few violent and terrifying seconds, Lydia is knocked aside and gored. Out of the swirling dust, her face and torso emerge to fill the screen, an almost sensual smile visible on her lips.[5]

We see her bleeding body being carried out by the men: in *Masurca Fogo* we will be reminded of it. Then we see a full-screen shot of the bull's insouciant face and head from the side. A mocker of man's enterprises, he is in the ceremony but not of it.

As real—and sometimes almost as deadly—as the loss of life is the loss of love, or of what for us counts as love. "Love is the saddest thing," Marco tells Lydia in the car to Córdoba, "when it goes away." Ten years after the end of his relationship with Lydia's predecessor, Angela, he is still mourning. When he kills a snake in Lydia's kitchen, he weeps because it reminds him of killing a different snake for Angela. Watching *Café Müller*, with Benigno—whom he has not yet met—sitting in the next seat, he weeps again, as he does for a third time, when he hears Caetano Veloso sing Tomás Méndez's ballad, "Cucurrucucú Paloma." His tears are important. Had the title not already been used by Sally Potter, Almodóvar would have called the film *The Man Who Cried*.[6] Tears can be misinterpreted, however, even when they are one's own.

In *Café Müller*, two distraught women stumble somnambulistically through an empty room. A man frantically moves chairs out of the way, trying to prevent the women from hurting themselves. His role is one with which Marco identifies. "I know nothing about bullfighting," he tells Lydia when he first meets her, "but a lot about desperate women." It is because he thinks she is desperate, indeed, that he wants to get to know her and write an "in-depth" article about her for the Sunday edition of *El País*. In that sense, his relationship with her is a sort of repetition— a replacement of one desperate woman with what he assumes to be another. Such women are as much his specialty as depressed or comatose ones are Benigno's. Even the books he reads are about them: on his bedside table, in the bedroom Benigno designed for Alicia, is a Spanish translation of Michael Cunningham's *The Hours*.[7]

When he first met Angela, she was a drug addict: "Angela and I traveled a lot," he explains to Lydia. "The excuse was to write a travel guide on some exotic place, but really it was to keep her away from drugs, to escape from Madrid. Life in Madrid was hell. Our relationship only worked when we got away." Eventually, however, he had to admit defeat: "After trying for five years and seven travel guides, I brought her here to Lucena, to her parents. They kept her away from drugs and from me." Again, the analogies with Benigno are striking. He becomes a nurse and beautician to take care of his mother; Marco becomes a travel writer to take care of Angela. In both cases, the relationships are somehow "special," to use Dr Roncero's word. They need their own isolated worlds in order to survive.

When Marco tells Lydia about Angela, the two have just seen her wedding ceremony. Lydia's first comment is telling: "I didn't think she was so *young*." It's a comment that the fairy tale quality of the ceremony may have prevented us from processing fully. But the emphasis on vows and consent seems intended to encourage us to be more alert.[8] The Angela we see—no signs of the desperate ex-addict showing through her blond and angelic exterior—cannot be over thirty (in fact, she looks no older than twenty-two or twenty-three). But that means that she was under fifteen when Marco met her. Though the age of consent in Spain was then twelve,[9] we have to wonder what sort of consent she—very young, addicted to drugs, far from home—could possibly have been capable of. We also have to wonder about Marco. What was *he* doing with *her*? What made her parents keep her away not just from drugs—succeeding where he failed apparently—but from him, too? Inside Benigno, there is something black, something that leads him to have sex with a comatose woman. Inside Marco, there also seems to be something black, something that smells bad, whatever name we choose to give it.

Watching Angela and Benjamin exchange vows, Marco's eyes, so prone to tears, remain dry. It's Lydia who weeps. Marco thinks he knows what that means: "You needn't worry. It's over with Angela. I've got proof. During the ceremony I didn't cry, but you did." In fact, her tears were not for him. They were for her Niño, with whom she had got back together a month earlier. *That* is what Lydia wants to talk about. But as their car pulls into Córdoba, she has yet to get a word in. For a month, Lydia's feelings have been elsewhere and Marco hasn't noticed. For an hour, he hasn't sensed her desire not just to listen, but to speak. Though he cannot bring himself to talk to her when she is comatose, she might as well have been comatose, we are shown, when he did talk to her.

In his relationship with Angela, it no doubt fell to Marco—older, richer, un-addicted—to be the dominant will. Maybe, too, it was a role that came naturally, as it does to Creon in Sophocles' *Antigone*. But its effect is to deprive others of agency and speech, to render them as-if comatose, as-if dead. Creon, notoriously, keeps the dead (Polynices) in the land of the living, while sending the living (Antigone) into the land of the dead. Angela may well have been as-if comatose already—another natural for the role in which she ended up being cast. But Lydia isn't like that. Her fear of snakes, which makes her seem Angela-esque to Marco, is just a phobia. She isn't a desperate woman who needs him to be her will. She has a will of her own. That's why she can leave him—or partly why.

Marco cries often. But sometimes, when we might expect him to, he doesn't. At *Café Müller*, watching the dancers and listening to Juno's lovely aria from Act 5 of Henry Purcell's *The Fairy Queen*, he does cry. The aria is about a woman desperate because her man is gone ("He's gone, he's gone, his loss deplore; And I shall never see him more.") The female dancers seem to express just that desperation. "Cucurrucucú Paloma" makes him cry, too. It is about a man weeping ("They say that at night he didn't do anything but cry") and dying ("calling out to her even as he died") over the loss of a woman. Marco's own killing of a snake also makes him cry. It is a case of a man helping a woman, desperate in the grip of a phobia. When Angela marries another man, however, he sheds no tears. When he discovers that Lydia had left him for Niño, again his eyes remain dry. No desperate woman, no man for him to identify with—no tears. Marco thinks he is crying over the loss of Alicia, but really he is crying over something else—over himself, perhaps, as her helper. We are as apt to be deceived as he.

The third and last time we see Benigno at his apartment window, he is holding Alicia's hairclip behind his back, opening and closing its suddenly ominous-looking teeth, watching for Alicia to arrive at the ballet school. She never comes. On a rainy Madrid street she was hit by a car. When we discover this, she has already been comatose in Woodland's for four years, with Lydia, also now comatose, down the hall. On the outside, the two women are much the same as before. Alicia, in particular, whose body is often visible, seems simply asleep. But what is inside? The potential deceptiveness of appearances, forever at issue in other areas in the film, has found its most humanly and philosophically disturbing locus. The bullfighter's costume hides the soft animal of the body. The dancer's costume hides it, too. Even the ballet lessons that shape it disguise it, making it look more powerful, more in control. What of the soft animal itself, then, that breathing, digesting, excreting, yawning, blinking, menstruating, ovulating thing? What does it hide? The person—perhaps incommunicado—within? The soul? Nothing?

In a discussion with Marco, Dr Vega, who is in charge of Lydia and Alicia, tries to answer this question:

MARCO: Is there no hope?

VERGA: As a doctor, I have to say no. However . . . (*He opens a magazine and shows it to Marco; the headline reads:* "Meryl Lazy Moon *awakens from a coma after 15 years.*") She went into a coma during childbirth. Meryl was a PVS, persistent vegetative state, like Lydia, theoretically unconscious for life. Her recovery contradicts all I'm about to say.

MARCO: So that means there is hope.

VERGA: No, I repeat, scientifically, no. But if you choose to believe, go ahead.

"I love the bullfighter's boyfriend," one of the nurses in the clinic says. "I bet you anything he's well hung . . . You can tell from a guy's face." "And especially from his crotch," the sardonic head nurse replies. Vega wants to sound equally hard-nosed and realistic. He wants to say that science sees the crotch. But he can't bring himself to do it. The face, he allows, can sometimes turn out—albeit miraculously—to be a better guide. Woodlands itself is testimony to wanting to have it both ways. A house of medicine, it would lose its *raison d'être* without the faith that medicine seems to exclude.

When Alicia is discovered to be pregnant, the attitude of the clinic's director exhibits none of this ambiguity. Addressing his staff, he says: "Our patient Alicia Roncero has been raped and is pregnant. I haven't told the father yet, because first you're going to tell me what bastard (*puta*) did that in my clinic." No one says now that her brain is dead, that she has no feelings, that the bastard was a necrophiliac, not a rapist. No one points out that the director himself has referred to Benigno as a "subnormal retard." The awfulness of what has happened precludes such niceties. Besides, the director is a thug and people's jobs and reputations are at stake.

Whatever befell Alicia a few months before that meeting, and whatever words best describe it, it is the seemingly black thing at the film's own center. It is one, however, that Almodóvar has purposely kept hidden from our view:

I treat the character Benigno as I would a friend. I see him neither from the point of view of normality nor of abnormality, only in terms of his near fanatical romanticism. He has his own logic, perfectly consistent with the world he lives in. In his world he is in control of everything, his own death even. I made a real effort not to judge the character, because I think that makes for a more interesting approach. Some might say that Benigno is a necrophiliac. That wouldn't necessarily be wrong. But I wanted to get away from all those sorts of categorizations. It was also my reason for including the film *The Shrinking Lover*: something is bound to happen to Benigno, I don't want to see it, nor do I want others to. It's like when a friend has done something terrible and you decide to turn a blind eye, just so as to keep them as a friend. I therefore came up with *The Shrinking Lover* in order to cover up what Benigno has done . . . But my desire to hide the wrong Benigno does is no doubt ambiguous, given that I place all the keys to unlock this secret inside the silent film, in which you can even guess how Benigno will end up.[10]

By giving us only indirect access to something that might otherwise overwhelm our intelligence, Almodóvar has acted like a judge who prevents the jury from seeing lurid photographs of the too-horribly tortured victim. In doing so, he takes a risk, of course, of having our imagination supply something yet worse than reality. But this he tries to offset by giving our intelligence a bone to chew on—*The Shrinking Lover*.

"I started going to the ballet on my days off," Benigno tells Marco in Alicia's room where they first meet. "And to the cinematheque. I try to see all the silent movies. German, American, everything. Then I tell her all I've seen. The last four years have been the richest of my life. Looking after Alicia, doing the things she liked to do, except traveling, of course." By entering Alicia's life, Benigno *has* genuinely enriched his own admittedly impoverished one in perhaps the only way possible: to live richly, he needs a rich role to enter into.[11] Then he sees *The Shrinking Lover*. Afterward, his face is harder, darker than before. For the first time, as he removes Alicia's gown to give her a massage, there is sexual tension in the air. He uncovers her breasts, then covers them again. "No, I'm all right," he says to himself, his eyes blinking. As he proceeds to recount the plot of the film, ironically turning something silent into words, we see the scenes he describes.

"Last night I saw a film that disturbed me," he tells her, "It was a love story between Alfredo, who's a bit overweight, like me, but a nice guy, and Amparo, his girlfriend, who's a scientist . . . working on an experimental diet formula." On the screen, full-frame, we see Amparo's words: "You're selfish. You only think of yourself." Alfredo's weight, we understand, symbolizes that selfishness; her formula, its cure. As soon as Amparo has a sample—"I've got it"—Alfredo grabs it. Although it is untested and potentially dangerous, he drinks it down. "Do you still think I'm selfish?" he asks. Immediately, he begins to shrink. As he does, the two kiss passionately: "It's done wonders for you," Amparo says. Unfortunately, he keeps on shrinking, until—when he is roughly the size of an erect penis—he magically stops. His selflessness has encountered the absolute barrier posed by the erotic life force (the love of fucking).

The psychological effects on Alfredo of getting smaller are represented as a return to his childhood home and his terrible mother. There, he eventually discovers a letter from his father telling him that if anything happened to him, it was his mother's fault. We see Alfredo reading it when he is escaping from home and mother, safe in Amparo's handbag. Their destination is Hotel Youkali—le pays du desir, the country of satisfied wishes.[12] Once there, they are soon in bed—Amparo naked, Alfredo in his underclothes. Amparo almost instantly falls asleep. (Female sexual wishes, to be satisfied, must remain hidden—waiting to be awakened by the right man. A woman who reveals them—especially in the 1920s, when the film is set—risks being thought loose, promiscuous, easy.) Alfredo gently pulls back the sheets, exposing Amparo's naked body. He climbs her breasts and lovingly embraces them. Then he discovers her pubic mound and vagina: "the most important thing," as Almodóvar calls it in his commentary. He puts his hand and arm inside her. When he withdraws it, it is wet and slippery with her secretions. He holds it to his face breathing in their intoxicating smell. A shot of her face shows us that she is aroused, even while asleep. Speaking its own natural language, the soft animal of her body has spoken its consent. When Marco says to Benigno that "Alicia can't say with any part of her body 'I do'," the odd formulation he employs focuses us on something he overlooks. Alicia is ovulating or close to it: she gets pregnant. As a result, there will be more mucus than usual in her vagina. We can imagine Benigno dis-covering this and (mis-)interpreting it—as Marco misinterprets Lydia's tears. Of course, Alicia and Amparo are crucially different: Amparo is an autonomous agent in a consensual relationship, who has undressed herself and taken Alfredo into her bed. If Alfredo interprets her wetness as a sign of consent, it is these facts that must serve as background for it. To Benigno, however, that difference is invisible. As the one who brings his beloved to life, he speaks for her as for himself. "Alicia's loving it," he says to Katerina about the Krzysztof Penderecki music she has put on—music that only he can hear.

Alfredo takes off his undershirt and puts the top half of his body inside Amparo. When he emerges, he is obviously aroused himself. He has become a doppelganger for the penis we never see. Again, Amparo's face shows her own answering arousal. Then Alfredo makes what is clearly a momentous decision. He removes his shorts and disappears inside her. As he does she climaxes, then returns contentedly to sleep. It has all been remarkably tender and non-violent—more an idyll of sex than the thing itself. We cut back to Benigno and Alicia. She is lying on her back, her eyes closed, her lips parted. He is on his knees by her bed, his right arm between her legs massaging her inner thigh upwards. His eyes are fixed on her vagina, hidden from us by the hem of her hitched-up gown. "And Alfredo," he says, his voice choking with emotion, "stays inside her forever." We see Alicia's face, again. Then the screen fills with a red phallic shape: it is a globule in the bedside lava lamp. Soon it thins out and divides, miming what we easily interpret as ejaculation and the fertilization of an ovum.

What arouses Benigno, what makes The Shrinking Lover so disturbing to him, it seems, is that it simultaneously brings into play elements that his strange life has kept artificially apart. When his father left, so did the man he himself should have become. As a result his style of loving got locked into the tender, non-genital (or aim-inhibited) form it took with his mother, never developing the forceful more aggressive component that would signal its successful amalgamation with male sexual desire. (The message from Alfredo's father engenders anger against the mother.) But non-genital love, for Benigno, is itself a strange thing: it consists in pouring his life force into the form of his beloved's life, putting life into her by immersing himself in her as in a role. Alfredo is overweight—selfish. There is a desire of Amparo's he hasn't satisfied—a desire that she can wordlessly express by getting wet. Only by becoming small, by becoming phallic, can he satisfy it, something he does by putting his entire life literally into her sleeping body. What is love for Benigno has found exactly the allegory of sex that it needs to become genital. When he enters Alicia, it is this new love that he is expressing—and as selflessly as he did its gentle non-genital predecessor. "You're incapable of hurting Alicia," Dr Vega says to him. "You can be sure of that," he replies. What he does, as always, he does for—what he imagines to be—her. It is in order to be united with her, indeed, that he takes the drugs, stolen from the prison infirm where he works: "I hope that all I've taken," he writes to Marco, "is enough to put me in a coma and reunite me with her." But he is not fated to be inside even that strange shared space with Alicia.

The coma he enters turns out to be death. The *pasión mortal* Caetano Veloso sings of has—in one of its many guises—claimed a victim.

When Benigno is in prison, charged with raping Alicia, the medical officer diagnoses him as a psychopath. Her father—too late—concurs: "They say it's good for the trial," Benigno tells Marco, "but I don't give a shit about that. I need to see Alicia and find out how it all ended." To the degree that we tend not to give a shit about it either, the risk that Almodóvar took with us has not paid off. Undistracted by the fancy play with *The Shrinking Lover*, we have insisted on seeing what it conceals as simply black and stinking. But this is one occasion in the film where not to judge by appearances is to miss something. "Benigno is insane," Almodóvar says, "but he has a good heart. He's a gentle psychopath."[13] The globule is red, not black.

The abrupt amalgamation of love and phallic sexuality that Benigno undergoes at the cinematheque—an homage, among other things, to the dangerous transformative power of film—is registered visually as a startling change in demeanor. It's as if he has become an adolescent male overnight. His beard is more visible. He's more foul-mouthed, ruder, more assertive. He dips big chunks of brioche into milk and shovels them into his mouth, like an uncouth teenager in need of table manners. One effect of this change is to bring his facial appearance closer to that of the swarthy Marco. When the latter visits him in prison for the first time, the camera exploits this similarity in order visually to impose his face on that of Benigno's and vice versa—something that the optical properties of the transparent barriers in the visiting room make possible. It is as if his voice comes from Benigno, Benigno's from him. It is also, at times, as if each is talking to himself—as if each is trapped in the "maze of mirrors" that Jean Vigo talks about, which yields only the image of his own image.[14] Though we are in the ventriloquist realm of what Benigno takes to be love, on what was a one-way street, perhaps for both parties, there is a closer approximation, at least, to traffic in both directions. Reading Benigno's letter, there in front of the impassive prison director, Marco sobs helplessly. This time, it seems, he is not only crying for himself.

Because of his trip, Marco has sublet his own apartment, so he rents Benigno's. Standing at the window where Benigno himself has often stood, he looks down into the ballet academy. To his shock and surprise, he sees Alicia. Though her son was stillborn, his birth has apparently precipitated her resurrection. The life Benigno put into her, first as an actor might, and then as semen might, seems finally to have become her own real life. The aura of fate and causation is palpable. But, really, it is just one of those accidents, like Lydia's name, that retrospectively takes it on. It doesn't redeem what Benigno did. It just allows it to have some good consequences.

The effect on Marco of inhabiting Benigno's life, of taking on his role, is represented as a new willingness to talk and to listen. "Talk to her," Benigno advises him, giving the film its actual title, but Marco can't: "I'd like to, but she can't hear me . . . because her brain is turned off." In his final letter, he gives the advice again: "Wherever they take me, come and see me, and tell me everything. Don't be so secretive." This time, though, even when the place to which Benigno is taken is the cemetery, Marco does pay attention: "Benigno, it's me," he says at the graveside, "Alicia is alive. You woke her up . . . I raced back to the jail to tell you, but it was too late. I put Alicia's hairclip in your pocket. And I also put in a photo of her and one of your mother, so that they'll be with you for all eternity." Benigno, it seems, has breathed a new life into him as well. As he places a bunch of red carnations on the tombstone, the music of the closing scene begins.

Marco is again crying at a Pina Bausch ballet, *Masurca Fogo*. Two rows behind him, unseen by him, are Alicia and Katerina. Things seem to have come full circle. On the stage, another distraught woman appears, borne horizontally along, as if on waves, by the upraised arms of a row of supine men. In her hands she holds a microphone, into which she lip-syncs kd lang singing Jane Siberry's "Hain't It Funny":

> We made love last night
> Wasn't good wasn't bad
> Intimate strangers made me kinda sad
> Now when I woke up this morning
> Coffee wasn't on
> It slowly dawned on me that my baby is gone
> My baby's gone.

As the song ends, she is raised aloft by the men then caught as she dives headlong down. "Cruel," Katerina comments to Alicia as they enter the foyer, "cruel waves. The male below, the female above." Is she thinking of waves of male desire that cause the woman's own desire to rise up, but leave her cruelly unsatisfied and abandoned? It's hard to know. But one thing seems certain, Katerina's interpretation isn't Marco's. For him, the ballet—with its desperate woman, lost male lover, rescuing male hands—is surely just another version of *Café Müller*. Though their disagreement is left implicit, it foreshadows one that will soon be out in the open.

Left sitting in the foyer, while Katerina goes to get water, holding the cane that she now needs to walk, Alicia notices Marco as he comes in from the auditorium. When he sees her, she returns his surprised gaze with something that looks almost like recognition—in love, a finding is always a re-finding.

As he sits smoking on the sofa across from her, she begins to talk to him, her voice deep and strong: "Are you all right?" She has sensed his emotional state, barely evidenced in his face and body language. The scene is a small one, handled with great restraint and delicacy. But something momentous happens in it. Instead of Marco responding to a woman's desperation, a woman has responded to his.

As if by sympathetic magic, the ballet's second act seems to continue the conversation Alicia has begun. From stage right, a line of male and female couples emerges, dancing now in harmony. Marco smiles, instead of crying, and turns to look at Alicia. Between them is an empty seat. It is the place of Benigno, we sense, who has brought them together, and then—like all good go-betweens—got out of the way. Alicia, her face bathed in beatific light, returns his smile. On the screen the legend "MARCO Y ALICIA" appears. Katerina, noticing the smile, turns anxiously toward Alicia, and impatiently redirects her attention to the stage. Marco, too, turns back, his face now joining Alicia's in the bright light of communion—of nascent love. On the stage, to which we ourselves are returned, the line of dancers breaks up, and all but two leave the stage. The woman walks in a pool of water in front of a towering wall of green vegetation. The man removes his panama hat and puts it on the ground by the pool's edge. As he keeps time with the woman's movements, he moves the hat along with his foot. Like the exchange in the foyer, the hat is a small thing—something put into the in-between, like a word in a conversation.

"I am alone," Marco tells Lydia, when she asks him if he's single. "I am alone," he repeats to the comatose Alicia after finding out that Lydia had returned to Niño. It is less a report of sexual status, we sense, than of existential condition. It isn't one that Almodóvar thinks to be especially his:

> When the psychiatrist asks Benigno what his problem is, he responds: "Loneliness, I suppose." Marco says to the two women he is with in the film at different periods that he is lonely. They do so without melodramatic flourish, simply stating the emptiness of their existence. Loneliness is something all the characters experience: Alicia and Lydia; Katerina, the dance teacher; Alicia's father . . . *Loneliness, I Suppose* is one of the possible titles for this film.[15]

The coma that isolates you can be inside you (Marco, Benigno, Dr Roncero) or you can be inside it (Alicia, Lydia). It hardly matters. If the first act of *Masurca Fogo* is the world of comatose isolation of either sort, the second can look awfully sunny—like the light in which Alicia and Marco are joined. It can look like Eden without the black snake.

New loves, of course, often look that way—especially to the lovers themselves. But we should be wise enough in the film's ways by now not to take things simply at face value. As Marco follows Alicia and Katerina back into the auditorium for the ballet's second act, Katerina, who met him at Woodlands, holds back. She wants to know what he said to Alicia. He reassures her that it was innocent. Then he tells her that if she sees him in her neighborhood, she shouldn't worry, since he lives across from her academy in Benigno's apartment:

KATERINA: Why are you living there?
MARCO: Benigno is dead.
KATERINA: (*shocked*) Oh! Oh! One day, you and I should talk.
MARCO: Yes, and it will be simpler than you think.
KATERINA: Nothing is simple. I'm a ballet mistress, and nothing is
simple.

These, the film's last words, sound another clear note of warning. The talk that she should have with Marco, Katerina sees, will have to deal with a complex history—with all that *Talk to Her* has shown us. But that history is much more than just what Marco and she will have to talk about; it is what Marco and Alicia will have to live with and work through—the missing black thing in *Masurca Fogo*'s Eden. Will Marco, killer of snakes, be up to the task? If he thinks it a relatively simple one, as he seems to, he has clearly taken in too much of Benigno—or been taken in too much by him. The small hat of hope that the film nudges toward us is that he won't have to do it alone. A lover of dance himself, he will have a dancer—and a ballet mistress—to help him. Maybe it will be enough.

Notes

1   A similar photograph appears in Almodóvar, *All About My Mother* (1999).
2   The date of Benigno's birth, shown on his tombstone in the penultimate scene, is 16–6–1972. That of his mother (Amelia Gomes) is 18–7–1930. She was 42 when he was born, and 62 when, 4 years before him, she died. Since he "lived twenty years day and night" with her, he was 5 when his 15 years of caretaking began, and 24 when he died.
3   Frederic Strauss (ed.), *Almodóvar on Almodóvar*, revised edition (London: Faber and Faber, 2006), p. 223.
4   Mary Oliver, "Wild Geese," in *Owls and Other Fantasies* (Boston: Beacon Press, 2003), p. 1.
5   The relationship between sex, orgasm, and death is explored in the context of bullfighting in Almodóvar's early film *Matador* (1986).
6   Paula Willoquet-Maricondi (ed.), *Pedro Almodóvar: Interviews* (Jackson: University Press of Mississippi, 2004), p. 163.
7   "On the cover you see a detail of painting of a body under water," Almodóvar comments, "with her hand resting on the water. This apparently casual image has a deep and complex resonance. On the one hand, this is a confession that I love *The Hours*, and that I would like to have made the movie, but they already did it. But it is also about the theme of death and water. Rain becomes for Benigno a point of entry into the world of Alicia's world coma." Willoquet-Maricondi, p. 167.
8   The only critic I know who has taken the cue is George Wilson, "Rapport, Rupture, and Rape: Reflections on *Talk to Her*," pp. 45–68, this volume, specifically pp. 60–1.
9   Established by the Criminal Code, enacted in 1995 (Article 181 f.). The Code also made it an offence, however, to seduce a person under 16 by deception or to violate the sexual liberty of a person of any age either through non-consensual sexual contact or through consensual contact obtained by taking advantage of a relationship of superiority that reduces sexual liberty. In 1999 the age of consent was raised from 12 to 13.
10 Strauss, p. 219.

11 "There was a dialogue I cut from the film in which his mother asks him: 'What will you do when I die?' He replies absolutely naturally, neither tragic nor provocative: 'I don't know—kill myself I suppose'." Strauss, pp. 216–17.

12 First introduced by Almodóvar in *Kika* (1993).

13 Strauss, p. 213.

14 "About a human being, one must, I believe, renounce ever reaching the reality of them . . . What anguish one feels in this race before a maze of mirrors, which only yield up the image of our own image, always of our own image." Quoted in Marina Warner, *L'Atalante* (London: British Film Institute, 1993), p. 77.

15 Almodóvar, *Hable con ella*, press book, 2002. Quoted in Martin D'Lugo, *Pedro Almodóvar* (Urbana: University of Illinois Press, 2006), p. 114.

Index

'Philosophers on Film' series
The Thin Red Line
Edited by David Davies

The Thin Red Line is the third feature-length film from acclaimed director Terrence Malick, set during the struggle between American and Japanese forces for Guadalcanal in the South Pacific during World War Two. It is a powerful, enigmatic and complex film that raises important philosophical questions, ranging from the existential and phenomenological to the artistic and technical.

This is one of the first collections dedicated to exploring the philosophical aspects of Malick's film. Opening with a helpful introduction that places the film in context, five essays, four of which were specially commissioned for this collection, go on to examine the following:

- the exploration of Heideggerian themes—such as being-towards-death and the vulnerability of Dasein's world—in *The Thin Red Line*
- how Malick's film explores and cinematically expresses the embodied nature of our experience of, and agency in, the world
- Malick's use of cinematic techniques, and how the style of his images shapes our affective, emotional, and cognitive responses to the film
- the role that images of nature play in Malick's cinema, and his 'Nietzschean' conception of human nature.

The Thin Red Line is essential reading for students interested in philosophy and film or phenomenology and existentialism. It also provides an accessible and informative insight into philosophy for those in related disciplines such as film studies, literature and religion.

ISBN 10: 0–415–77364–4 (hbk)
ISBN 10: 0–415–77365–2 (pbk)

ISBN 13: 978–0–415–77364–5 (hbk)
ISBN 13: 978–0–415–77365–2 (pbk)

Philosophy Goes To The Movies
(Second Edition)
Christopher Falzon

- What can we learn about the nature of knowledge from *Rear Window*?
- How can *Total Recall* help us understand personal identity?
- What does *High Noon* have to do with Kant?

From *Metropolis* to *The Matrix*, from *Gattaca* to *Groundhog Day*, films can help to illustrate and illuminate complex philosophical thought.

Philosophy Goes to the Movies is a new kind of introduction to philosophy that makes use of film to help us understand philosophical ideas and positions. Drawing on a wide range of films from around the world, and the ideas of a diverse selection of thinkers from Plato and Descartes to Marcuse and Foucault, Christopher Falzon introduces and discusses central areas of philosophical concern, including the theory of knowledge, the self and personal identity, ethics, social and political philosophy, and critical thinking.

Ideal for beginners, this book guides the reader through philosophy using lively and illuminating cinematic examples including *A Clockwork Orange*, *Mulholland Drive*, *Blade Runner*, *Modern Times* and *Wings of Desire*.

ISBN 10: 0–415–35725–X (hbk)
ISBN 10: 0–415–35726–8 (pbk)

ISBN 13: 978–0–415–35725–8 (hbk)
ISBN 13: 978–0–415–35726–5 (pbk)

On Film
(Second Edition)
Stephen Mulhall

Reviews of the first edition:

'Mulhall's philosophical discussion of each film is highly stimulating. A provocative and engaging book which makes for stimulating reading for anyone interested in both film and philosophy.'

Matthew Kieran, *Philosophical Books*

'The themes he identifies as central—most crucially, a concern with human embodiment and thus, with both human generativity and mortality—are explored convincingly, even brilliantly at times . . . Despite the amount of closely argued material which is packed into a relatively short book, the clarity and precision of the writing make it something of a page-turner.'

Deborah Thomas, *European Journal of Communication*

In this significantly expanded new edition of his acclaimed exploration of the relation between philosophy and film, Stephen Mulhall broadens the focus of his work from science fiction to the espionage thriller and beyond.

The first part of the book discusses the four *Alien* movies. Mulhall argues that the sexual significance of the aliens themselves, and of Ripley's resistance to them, takes us deep into the question of what it is to be human. These four chapters develop a highly original and controversial argument that films themselves can philosophize—a claim Mulhall expands upon and defends in part two of this book, before applying his interpretative model to another sequence of contemporary Hollywood movies: the *Mission: Impossible* series.

A new chapter is devoted to each of the three films in that series, discussing them in the context of other films by the relevant directors. In this discussion, the nature of television becomes as central a concern as the nature of cinema; and this shift in genre also makes room for a detailed reading of Spielberg's *Minority Report*.

On Film, Second Edition is essential reading for anyone interested in philosophy, film theory and cultural studies, and in the way philosophy can enrich our understanding of cinema.

Stephen Mulhall is Fellow and Tutor in Philosophy at New College, Oxford, and author of *Heidegger and Being and Time* (Routledge) and *The Conversation of Humanity*.

ISBN: 0–41544153–6 (hbk)

ISBN: 978–0–415–44153–7 (pbk)
ISBN: 978–0–203–92852–3 (ebk)

Thinking on Screen
Film as Philosophy
Thomas E. Wartenberg

'This book is a powerful defense of the view that films can philosophize. Characterized by its clear and lively presentation, and by its inter-twining of philosophical argument with detailed discussion of several important films, it will be of interest not just to those studying philosophy and film but to everyone who believes in the importance of film to our cognitive life.'

Berys Gaut, *University of St Andrews*

Thinking on Screen: Film as Philosophy is an accessible and thought-provoking examination of the way films raise and explore complex philosophical ideas.

Beginning with a demonstration of how specific forms of philo-sophical discourse are presented cinematically, Wartenberg moves on to offer a systematic account of the ways in which specific films undertake the task of philosophy. Focusing on the films *The Man Who Shot Liberty Valance, Modern Times, The Matrix, Eternal Sunshine of the Spotless Mind, The Third Man, The Flicker* and *Empire*, Wartenberg shows how these films express meaningful and pertinent philosophical ideas.

Thinking on Screen: Film as Philosophy is essential reading for students of philosophy with an interest in film, aesthetics and film theory. It will also be of interest to film enthusiasts intrigued by the philosophical implications of film.

Thomas E. Wartenberg is Professor at Mount Holyoke College and author of *Unlikely Couples: Movie Romance as Social Criticism* and *The Forms of Power.*

ISBN 10: 0–4157730–6 (hbk)
ISBN 10: 0–41577431–4 (pbk)
ISBN 10: 0–20303062–1 (ebk)

ISBN 13: 978–0–415–77430–7 (hbk)
ISBN 13: 978–0–415–77431–4 (pbk)
ISBN 13: 978–0–203–03062–2 (ebk)

Available at all good bookshops
For ordering and further information please visit:
www.routledge.com